The Barry John Story

Barry John was the greatest fly-half of his generation; among the greatest the game has ever produced. In terms of points scored his achievement was phenomenal – yet it is not by statistics that he would wish to be judged, but by what he gave to rugby. He will be remembered for his speed, the sureness of his handling, the incredible anticipation which enabled him to see not one, but two or three, moves ahead of his opponents; his deceptively casual but deadly kicking, his courage, his tenacity, above all, perhaps, for his sportsmanship. He played rugby because he loved it; and though he played fiercely to win, victory was never the be-all and end-all of his game.

In this book he tells of his youth in a Welsh mining village. In his childhood, he says, 'I seemed always to be kicking a ball . . . And I could not spy a piece of waste paper, or a cigarette-end, or a piece of wood, without running up and aiming a kick at it – and hearing in my imagination, the roar of an appreciative crowd.' And so from school and village rugby he moved to Llanelli, to Cardiff, and to the red jersey of Wales. The rest is history. Vividly he recounts the triumphs of the Welsh team in the early 1970s, the Lions' tour of South Africa in 1968, the disastrous Welsh visit to New Zealand in 1969; and the crowning glory of 1971 when the British Lions beat the All Blacks by two matches to one.

D1614853

The
Barry John
Story

—

by Barry John

Collins

ST JAMES'S PLACE, LONDON

1974

William Collins Sons & Co Ltd
London · Glasgow · Sydney · Auckland
Toronto · Johannesburg

First published 1974
Reprinted January 1974
Reprinted February 1974
© Barry John 1974
ISBN 0 00 216011 0

Set in Monotype Baskerville
Made and printed in Great Britain by
William Collins Sons & Co Ltd Glasgow

TO JAN

I would like to record my special thanks
to my friend Trevor Fishlock who helped
greatly in the preparation of this book

Contents

Illustrations

1. The Red Jersey

I only wish that my Uncle Lloyd had lived to see me take that last, record-breaking penalty kick at Cardiff Arms Park, in front of that huge crowd. He had been a typical Welsh rugby fan – which is to say that he was nutty about the game. Just to mention rugby in his hearing was to turn on a tap of words and excitement. He was endlessly discussing last week's match, and the prospects for the next one, in a flood of language peppered with swear words. He was packed with knowledge about players and had instant recall of incidents in matches years back. When his local team in the Carmarthenshire valley where we lived was winning, he was loud and exuberant on the touchline; when it was making a mess of things he would smack his fist into his palm with great ringing groans, or he would throw his cap down in the mud, or else he would sing at the top of his voice to give encouragement.

He was like so many thousands of us in Wales: rugby football was one of the big slices of his life. It was as much a part of the colour of his background and upbringing as coal mining. He died, though, without ever seeing me play for Wales. If he could have seen his own sister's boy, one of his family, running out on to that Arms Park turf in the red jersey, he would have glowed like a lamp with pride.

I put the ball down and retreated my usual three paces to take the kick.

It was my twenty-fifth match for Wales. We were playing France on one of those bright cold days in March and in the crowd were Red Dragons and tricolours and the sounds of the 'Marseillaise' and 'Land of My Fathers.' We were given this penalty about ten minutes after half-time and the ball was thirty-five yards out from the posts. The noise had fallen to a chatter and then a buzz. Everyone in the stadium knew that with this kick I had a chance to beat Jack Bancroft's points record for Wales which had stood for fifty-eight years.

I didn't worry about it; I wouldn't let myself. I ran up and banged the ball with my instep and watched it soar – and thought, hell, I've missed it. It looked for an instant as if it were swinging away from the post. I turned and bit on my lower lip. But the shout from the crowd brought my eyes round again. The ball was there. I had scored ninety points for Wales.

There was at once an elation, a relief, a sadness. It was a most curious sensation. A couple of my team-mates jogged up to pat my shoulder. Others gave a nodded 'Well done.' I was on top of the world, with the crowd roaring. But I knew that when this match was ended I would run off for the last time as a Welsh player.

Only a few people in the ground – my family, a few team-mates and Gerry Lewis, the physiotherapist – knew that I was really drawing the line with that penalty kick. I was twenty-seven years old and at the peak of my career at the very top of world rugby. I was young enough to have the prospect of perhaps three or four more seasons in the first-class game. But I was going – and my decision was irrevocable.

I had worried for months over this decision to retire. Wherever I was and whatever I was doing, the matter was always on my mind. So that once I had decided – and I knew in my bones I was right – there was a sense of relief.

We beat the French by twenty points to six and I had scored four penalties. Two of them were among the best shots of my career. We went off, shaking hands and slapping shoulders and smiling, with people crowding around us. Being in a winning team is a great feeling and I knew I was going to miss it – and everything about playing first-class rugby – a lot.

To play for Wales has been the dream or ambition of thousands of boys, and it remains so.

One night, when my brother Alan and I were small boys, we went to bed after a hard game in the park and I said: 'One day I shall play for Wales.'

'Go to sleep,' Alan said, turning over, 'and don't talk so daft.'

In our part of the world rugby is *the* game. I can't be sure why a game that started off in English public schools was taken up by the working class in the mining valleys of South Wales with such enthusiasm, but it has become a fundamental part of our tradition and heritage.

In even the most narrow and tortuously twisted valleys, where the houses have to hang on to the mountainsides, room has always been scraped out for a rugby pitch.

And rugby itself, tough and fast, a man's game with its own controlled violence, its special skills and lore, its combination of brain and muscle, the emotional involvement of watchers and watched, has always appealed strongly to the Welsh temperament. It may be that through rugby many thousands of men who spent their lives in cramped darkness underground found a much-needed expression of vigour and action and freedom in the open air. It is also an expression of our nationality and it is one way in which a small country can make itself noticed.

And, of course, in a country whose people have a bit of a reputation for forming committees at the drop of a hat, a rugby team is a pretty formidable committee!

Whatever the source of rugby's magic, it usually starts working at an early age. If a small boy announces that he's going to play for Wales it usually means just one thing. Rugby.

And I can assure you that the reality matches up to the boyhood fantasy. No wonder I was going to miss it.

It is a supreme experience, a ride on a kind of magic carpet. And the first thing you get is the ticket. This is a white card, bearing a three-feathers crest; it comes in a little Sellotaped parcel from the Welsh Rugby Union and it invites you to play for Wales.

The first four times I received the white card it bore the word Reserve in brackets after my name. I used to put my thumb over the word and imagine that I really was going to play. But I had to wait.

The white card comes ten days before the match and you casually put it on the mantelpiece where you, and everyone else for that matter, can see it. You don't tire of the sight of it. You see it just before you switch the light off when you go up to bed and you see it when you come down again in the morning.

The next thing is the smell of rugby.

I've known it since I was a small boy and it still makes my flesh tingle with anticipation and excitement. It is a sporty, masculine, sharp smell: wintergreen, Vaseline, grass, mud and maybe a little sweat. If it's too strong it makes your eyes water. It makes Jan, my wife, wrinkle her nose.

During the night before the big matches, Gerry Lewis used to come to the hotel room I shared with Gareth Edwards to give us a massage to relax and trim our muscles. He rubbed on the wintergreen mixture and the room used to smell of it. Heaven knows what the chambermaids thought when they came round to change the sheets. It is a smell that seems to stick to the walls.

I remember the smell of the old Llanelli dressing room at Stradey Park: a grubby and yellowed room, though it was supposed to be red and white, the club colours. It had one door and no air seemed to pass through it. It wasn't filthy but it had the sort of comfortable and pleasant and familiar dirt that we liked. Everything stank and the wintergreen and the Vaseline seemed to ooze out of the walls. A fly couldn't live there.

You went in there and it meant rugby, sport, action. It meant – let's get changed, let's get out there and show them. You flexed your muscles. It was a warm and electrifying room and I used to love it. Modern dressing rooms don't retain the smell so much. I mean, they are tiled and plastic and you can wipe them clean so that you would hardly know rugby footballers had been in them. That wood-panelled room at Llanelli had bits of the club history ingrained in the timber. Those cracks and splinters filled with mud and Vaseline and paint bore the marks of past players. The place where you hung your shirt was the place where, years before, a mighty forward had thrown a great punch at the wall in a fearsome temper and had split the panelling and had gone down in the lore of the club.

I not only miss rugby's aromas. I miss, too, the feeling of walking on air, of slowly winding up the spring in the days before an international match.

Before 1969 the Welsh squad used to meet for training on Fridays, but that wasn't a good day because if you got a bruise or a knock only twenty-four hours before the match you could be in trouble. Sensible squad training two days before the match was a much better idea. So we would meet up at three o'clock at the police sports ground in Bridgend for seventy minutes of training. Clive Rowlands, the coach, is firm, but not hard, and made sure the players left the session thoroughly exercised, but not shattered. The backs and forwards trained separately for most of the session and then we would combine for about fifteen minutes of unopposed rugby.

On Thursday evenings I would go home. That way the game seemed far away and I could relax more easily. And next day I would go to work as usual in Cardiff. I was working at that time for the Forward Trust finance house, as an executive, and at lunchtime went out for a large meal with three or four friends from the office. I could rely on their keeping the conversation light; not too much talk about rugby. I wouldn't eat anything rich, just plainly served steaks, chops or fish, with chips. Then I went back to work until about half past four and drove the five miles to home in Radyr for some tea and to change into casual clothes and pack my bag and my boots.

I used to arrive at the Angel Hotel, which is a hundred yards from Cardiff Arms Park, about six o'clock. Other players were there, or just arriving, and an atmosphere of expectation began to develop.

Routine, and even a little ritual, is important at times like this. There is nothing like predictability when you are becoming keyed up for a big occasion. The pattern altered little. We used to go to our rooms and then be summoned to Gerry's room to be given our stockings, shorts and the reimbursement of our expenses. We were also given our tickets for the Saturday night dance which follows every match.

By now we would all be chattering a lot and ribbing each other about the performances of our home clubs and by half past seven we would be heading for the section of the hotel dining-room reserved for us.

If you want to know something of a rugby side's team spirit – the magic ingredient – observe the way the players behave when they enter the dining-room. If they sit around in small knots something is wrong. The important thing about the Welsh side – certainly in my experience – was that we always felt and thought as a team. No man ever sat alone at a table. If a man was first in the room he would soon be joined by others. And if two players occupied a table the other two places would quickly be filled. Playing, or eating, we wanted to work together.

This dinner was an important one. We did not know the meaning of the word snack and we always ate very well. The chef knew that he was dealing with men of appetite. I usually started with pâté and then had a steak, or, like some of the other boys, two steaks if I was really hungry. Plenty of vegetables and chips – but never more than one glass of wine.

After this feast we assembled in the foyer. Sometimes there might be a match at the Cardiff club ground next to the Arms Park and we would go over and watch it. But usually a trip to the pictures was arranged. The people in the cinema must have wondered what was happening when this crowd of young men came, in, some of them very bulky and broad-shouldered who had to shoe-horn themselves into the seats. In the interval there was always ice-cream for everybody in the party. And we returned to the hotel relaxed and in a good temper.

A room was set aside for us, with plenty of coffee, tea, milk – and a small mountain range of sandwiches. After all that film-watching we were ravenous. The sandwiches usually vanished pretty smartly, amid laughter, along with the shreds of lettuce and cress garnish.

After this it was time to go to our rooms. Gareth, who always shared with me, usually took some milk with him. Other players used to call for coffee or tea, for it was too early to go to sleep. Gareth and I would watch television in our room until Gerry came in between midnight and one o'clock. He always gave us a thorough massage, laughing and chatting all the time, and he left us tingling and full of well-being, like kids tucked up on Christmas Eve. It's a great way to go to bed.

I always woke up first, about half past eight, and went to the window to see what the weather was like. Then I picked up the telephone to order breakfast: tea for two, toast **and** marmalade for me, toast and honey for Gareth, and the morning papers, to read what the sports writers were saying about the match.

After breakfast, Gareth would get on the telephone to make sure that various friends had received tickets. Now tickets can be the bane of a player's life: everyone imagines that you can get your hands on dozens of them and people say: 'If you can't get them, who can?'

I know perfectly well that tickets for the big matches take on some of the aura and scarcity of nuggets of Welsh gold, but the fact is that each player gets just two complimentary tickets (when I played it was one) – and he'll probably give that to his wife or his father or his best friend – and he has the option to buy two stand tickets in the £1.50 range and a few enclosure and ground tickets. So I had five or six tickets and I paid for all but one.

There are many pressures on players over tickets – and I suppose that they caused me more worry than anything else in rugby.

Players just cannot get enough of them to meet the demands. Take my own case: people have been very good to me throughout my life and they have given help without a thought of reward. But if I can give someone a ticket to an international it is a very positive way of saying thank you.

My family never asked for tickets. They understood the situation and my in-laws, in any case, have debenture tickets at the Arms Park.

I believe there is a need for a better, a more generous, tickets system, so that players are not saddled with worries. They shouldn't have to endure it. I remember one player who was making his first appearance for Wales and was absolutely besieged. Naturally all his family and friends wanted to see him on his big day. He was so worried about it that I became a bit angry and turned shop steward and persuaded the Welsh Rugby Union to provide a few more tickets; and from that time the situation has improved a little.

Anyway, I soon made a firm rule for myself: I would have nothing to do with tickets after the Tuesday before the match. And that was a great relief.

After Gareth had sorted himself out, there was another ritual.

He and I would walk to the shops to buy him a shirt. In some of the shops the assistants would not recognise us and, as a part of their patter as we looked over the selection of shirts, they would ask: 'Going to the match today, sir?' And we would answer: 'Mm, might do. If the weather stays nice.'

Back at the Angel there was now quite an atmosphere, a building up of excitement, with people chattering noisily and packing tightly around the bar. Players and officials were talking to their wives and friends – and boys were wriggling through the crowd to get autographs.

At half past eleven the call went out: 'Team meeting!'

For some reason this was usually held in the half-backs' room – and I used to dash up and stow my stuff away before the others got there. It wasn't that I didn't trust my team-mates. But if a well-built front-row forward stands on one of your shoes it is not likely to be worth wearing afterwards.

The boys went into the room. They were confident, but, with the match just a few hours off they had the right and necessary edge of nervousness.

Clive, the coach, put his first cigarette into his lips and looked around, seeing if anyone was missing. If anyone scrambled in late he wagged his finger . . . 'I'm bloody well warning you.'

Then, with deliberate slowness and care, he would step up the tension and the urge to get into action. It's a technique that clever sergeants might have used before ordering their men over the top.

The room is full and all the bodies in it are pressing close together and each man watches the coach intently. Body heat warms the room and Clive's smoke fugs it.

He calls Gareth out and says: 'Right, Gareth, here's the scrum. Serious, now, boys.'

There's no scrum and no ball, yet every man in that room would swear there was. Gareth says: 'Steady, Jeff. And NOW!'

He's crouched down and Clive is crouched down with him.

Clive says: 'Not good enough, boys. Let's try it again.'

Gareth shoots the imaginary ball into the imaginary scrum.

'Jeff – now!' And the forwards start shouting and straining forward as if they really are out there in front of the crowd.

Clive starts another cigarette. 'That's better, now.' The temperature in the room is rising and Clive starts to talk rapidly and the tension becomes immense.

There is always a story: it varies in detail but it is basically the same. It is about a group of Welshmen who have made a long journey, and have encountered obstacles, just to watch us play. Clive tells us, then repeats how fortunate we are to play for Wales, how any one of the thousands in the crowd would give five years' pay to run out with us in the red jersey.

His voice grips us. 'Now think of all your friends and your families and the people you work with. Depending on you. They've travelled and saved up to watch you, or else they're in front of their televisions or radios just willing you to win. They don't want you to win just for yourselves. They want you to win for Wales. You are playing for your country. You are representing Wales. You are very lucky. In your local pubs, in pubs throughout Wales, there's a special extension till five in the morning. But only if you win. Only if Wales wins.'

In the electric silence he fixes his eyes on one player and the ash falls from his cigarette. He begins to raise his voice. 'Now we are not afraid of anybody. We are the best rugby team in Europe. Wales is the best. We have proved it before and we shall prove it again this afternoon. We are going to tackle and pass like we've never done before. And we are going to win – .' He shoots out a finger. 'What are we going to do?'

The player fixed in his gaze says: 'We are going to win.'

Clive says loudly: 'What?'

'Win.'

'Louder.'

A whole chorus comes back at him. 'WIN!'

'That's right,' Clive says, breathing hard, a new cigarette puffing. 'We will win, for our families and for Wales.' He puts his hand over his heart. 'I can feel it. My heart is going like mad. We are going to win. What are we going to do?'

'Win! Win!'

And now we are a moulded force of men. The forwards

hang on Clive's every word and their eyes are bright. They are absolutely keyed for action; like dogs waiting for the leashes to be slipped.

Clive makes a quick joke. Some of the tension subsides, like air hissing from a bulging balloon. The session is over and we go down to our lunch.

Usually I ordered a steak and performed the same routine with it. I would cut six small squares of the meat, eat them and leave everything else. Then I would go up to our room to watch television.

If the kick-off was at three o'clock we had to be in the dressing room by two. I usually went over with Gareth. In the dressing room there was another ritual, so important that we would have thought things were terribly wrong if it had not taken place.

Gerry the physio, a slight man in track suit trousers and singlet, was there with his long kit bag, rather like a cricket bag. Inside it were the new red shirts.

Gerry would approach each player and solemnly hand over a shirt and shake hands. He would say: 'Well done, you deserve it.' It did not matter if it was your first match or your twenty-first match; he always made the ceremony of the shirt something special – and I look back on it with appreciation. I would take the shirt and flick it to open it out and to see the number ten on the back. It was always a thrilling moment – and I can remember other players, playing for Wales for the first time, inflating their chests and glancing down at the coveted jersey: Christmas, birthday and a pools win rolled into one great moment.

By then it was time to go out and sniff the air in the stadium. We were greeted by a roar from the crowd and that used to make us feel elated: a good home crowd is worth five points and sometimes an extra man. I used to note the strength of the breeze and the state of the turf and file away the information in my brain.

Back in the dressing room I would have a massage on the table while Gerry talked quietly. Without him there would be a lot missing from Welsh rugby. He's a sort of daddy, or uncle, to the players. He is very calm, never raises his voice or gets flustered and he knows the idiosyncrasies of the players. He knows the men who will fret if they have to wait for a massage and those who will happily queue.

After my rub I would dress, always pulling on the right stocking and right boot first. A proper nervousness would have us making fairly frequent visits to the urinal. There's a wonderful, a slightly nerve-racking tension. We would dash out for the team photograph and then come back.

Suddenly all officials, selectors, members of the Welsh Rugby Union, would disappear and we would be left alone, with the minutes ticking by. A few players don't put on their boots until the last possible moment. They want to lace up and run out, no hanging about.

We felt as boxers must feel when they are at last left alone in the ring and they have to get on with the fighting.

Then Fred Croster, a former rugby referee, who assists in the dressing room and keeps the players buoyed up with words of encouragement, would come in.

'Lads, it's time.'

Except when I was vice-captain of Wales, and had to run out behind the skipper, I always tried to run out with Gareth. The policemen at the entrance to the tunnel give thumbs-up signs and murmur encouragement.

At that moment you feel super-fit. If you had an ache or a bruise or a stuffy nose beforehand it has all gone now. You feel tall, tense, invincible. Just putting on that red jersey has chased away every little pain and germ.

I always made a point of handling the ball before the match started. To the spectators a ball may be simply a ball, but to the players, and particularly the kickers, the quality of the ball is important. I would always pick up the ball and place one end of it against my chest, squeezing it against my body. If it was a hard, or a soft, ball I would have to vary my method of kicking. An over-inflated ball has a distinctive 'ping' when kicked; a soft one, a distinctive thud.

In both cases they are not so easy to flight as a correctly inflated ball, and to counteract the fault I would kick across the seam. When a ball was thrown in to replace a match ball kicked over the stand, I always tried to handle it briefly, just to get an idea of its character. All this may sound rather finicky, but it pays to take pains – the information goes into the memory to augment instinct – and small precautions can make the difference between a snap dropped-goal and a groan from the crowd. I remember our match in Paris in 1969 when I told the referee that the ball had gone soft. He agreed and it was replaced, but when the replacement was kicked out the soft ball was returned to the field. Keith Jarrett had a shot at goal with it, but he had no hope of scoring with a ball like that.

Before I tossed the ball away I always rubbed it against the toe of my boot . . . introduced it to my foot. It was a little bit of superstition that made me feel better.

On the field, I always grabbed a handful of soil and

rubbed it into my hands, not just to improve my grip, but to disguise the strapping around my hands. I had to tape my hands carefully before each match because my thumbs are easily dislocated. That should have been safe enough, but once, when I was playing for Llanelli, I was in the thick of a rather bad-tempered ruck and an opponent grabbed my hand and twisted it. I felt he had been attracted to my vulnerable spot by the white tape. After that I decided to remove temptation from opposing forwards and camouflage the tape with mud.

I was fortunate to be in top-class rugby at a time when the game was going through a renaissance, if not a transformation. The Welsh team, in particular, embarked on a new golden age. The ruling of 1968 which limited kicking into touch – you could no longer kick into touch outside your own twenty-five yard line – was an important contribution to the enhancement of rugby for spectators and players alike. This rule changed rugby almost overnight. Before it came into force a player didn't have to think too hard; but under the new law players and coaches had to think carefully. The result of their training, and their thinking on and off the field, has made rugby into one of the world's most exciting team games. It has become more fluid and open and, when everything clicks, a more beautiful game.

Great coverage on television has brought more people into contact with rugby and in the past three or four years the game has caught on with the British public in a way it never has before. But, of course, it's not simply a question of television: the game itself has become more spectacular.

The five-nil, nine-six, international scores are almost a thing of the past. Now it's more likely to be twenty-twelve, thirty-fifteen, with the penalty kick being cancelled out by a magnificent try and plenty of cut and thrust.

Rugby is a complex game but many thousands, who can never be sure why the whistle goes, enjoy watching the action, following the ball and the patterns of movement. Many women have become attracted to the game: they love the battles and they love to see the contests between the seventeen-stone forward and the eleven-stone half-back or centre. David v. Goliath. The contests are primitive and clear-cut. The smaller player with the ball is in constant danger and he must have wit and speed to break through; if the big player has the ball everyone can see that the smaller player, heading him off and tackling him, needs a lot of courage.

Quite apart from the fundamental brains versus brawn aspect of rugby, there is plenty to occupy the connoisseur. The subtleties and mistakes provide him with enough material for argument over many drinks for weeks to come. And many more people – thanks partly to good television – are getting to know more about the game.

A small indication of rugby's new wave of popularity was that John Dawes, the Welsh skipper, and I got into the top ten of a number of sports polls in 1971–2 and that more top rugby players became known to the general public. My appearance as the subject of a *This is Your Life* programme, when the British Lions returned in triumph from New Zealand in 1971, not only promoted me but, more important in my view, it promoted rugby football.

The Barry John Story

While rugby's new wave was gathering momentum, I was right on the crest of it, at the peak of my fitness and skill.

And all of rugby – all of its rituals and tensions, the sheer physical exultation of being fast and fit, the pleasure of winning, of being part of great teams, of playing for my country, of travelling and having fun – I have found so very hard to give up.

Naturally I loved to hear the crowd applauding and I liked to have my shoulder patted and it was pleasant to be recognised. I don't suppose there are many of us who do not enjoy some appreciation of our efforts. But what began to depress me – and, in the end, to frighten me – was the intensifying public movement towards my own deification.

I became famous and I must admit that I liked it – up to a point. But people began to put me on a pedestal and writers started calling me 'a legend in his own lifetime' – a phrase that gave me the creeps, perhaps because it seemed to wrap me up and file me away. I had no wish to be a legend; I wanted to be me. I am a perfectly ordinary individual from an ordinary background. And while I am fortunate enough to have a gift for playing rugby football I don't have much talent for coping with hyper-adulation and its suffocating side-effects.

Let me make myself clear: I don't want to sound ungrateful or selfish or arrogant and I don't want to upset anyone. Rugby has helped me enormously and has given my life a fabulous dimension. After all, I was a teacher and I enjoyed teaching, but I could not have lived the life I do today, even in the purely material sense, on a teacher's salary. Rugby has given me many things, people have

done much for me and the rugby ball has certainly
bounced very kindly for me.

But, boy, has it brought pressures.

At first it was all fun. What boy wouldn't be tickled at
the sight of his name in the local paper? And it was there
almost every week in the *Carmarthen Journal* when I played
for Cefneithin and Llanelli. It was fun when I began
playing for Wales. But in the last year of my playing
career, and particularly when I got back from New
Zealand, the pressures became more than I could stand.

As my playing life developed I found that people, at
first by the dozen, and then the score, wanted to shake my
hand and slap my shoulder. That was fine, and I revelled
in it. But then more people wanted to prod my chest, pull
my hair, tug my clothes and take my shirt buttons. In a
crowd there were always fingers in my back.

In New Zealand, with the Lions, I had the nickname of
'King' and the adulation began to swell to such a pitch
that, knowing human nature and knowing how much
rugby meant to people in Wales, I began to worry about
the reception I would get when we returned home.

This feeling grew more intense after the third Test at
Wellington where we beat the All Blacks thirteen points to
three. It was a historic match and there was some
magnificent rugby. The Lions were really heroes now and
Clem Thomas, *The Observer*'s rugby writer, said to me:
'Barry, you'll just have to live with this fame for the rest of
your life.'

When I got home the invitations came in thick and
fast: to dinners, lunches, meetings, parties, receptions, all
kinds of social events. The former simplicity of my life
was suddenly altered. I dislike disappointing people and I

knew that I owed the Welsh rugby supporters an unpayable debt for their goodwill and support and, in this time of great triumph for Welsh rugby, I felt a duty to go out and meet as many people as possible.

But somehow, in some mysterious metamorphosis, I had been changed from a rugby player into a star.

There was an endless round of personal appearances and I had invitations from societies, clubs and organisations of all kinds, about thirty invitations a week. I even had one from a budgerigar society!

My home life began to suffer and I became a lodger in my own house, darting in to put on a clean shirt before hurrying off to the next engagement. To an extent my wife and little daughter became strangers. Jan said to me several times: 'Why don't you talk to me any more?' But I hardly knew what she meant.

She no longer said: 'What would you like for dinner tonight?' But: 'When are you home next?'

I was in a bad mood half the time and could barely bring myself to utter more than a grunt or two at home. I'm afraid that personal life went out of the window to such an extent that, if my wife had fallen down the stairs and broken a leg, it would have taken a few days for me to realise what had happened.

I was getting home at one or two o'clock in the morning, going off to do a day's work and then spending the evening at a function. I was lucky to be working for an understanding employer and to have the services of a secretary at my office who looked after the mail and took a load from my shoulders. Without such help I could not, as an amateur player, have conducted my life with any order at all.

I had hoped that in my working life I would have been able to talk about finance – it would have been relaxing and it was, after all, my business. But conversations nearly always turned to rugby, as they did everywhere else.

Eventually I grew to loathe talking about rugby. I developed the knack of giving an after-dinner type of speech to suit any kind of occasion, but after that I did not want to discuss the game. Everywhere I went people buttonholed me and brought up the hated subject – 'How did you get that penalty? That try? What was X like?' – endless inanities. Some people used to ask me the colour of the Welsh jersey.

I began to scream inwardly. I craved conversation about other topics and I was grateful to the few people who, when they approached for a chat, steered clear of rugby. I disliked having to analyse events in matches, to analyse my own talent and motives. I kicked for touch, ran in this direction or that, simply because I am an instinctive player and, in the split-second of decision in the heat of the action, the moves seemed to be the obvious or the best ones at the time. How could I analyse the moves, days or weeks later, at the end of a tiring evening?

I began to feel guilty that this was my reaction. Taking part in small-talk I could hear the words leaving my lips, but they were processed and said without feeling. I began to feel I was cheating people, that I did not care, that I was dishonest and that I had been turned into a kind of circus act.

The quantity of the demands upon me was increasing. I began to feel that They were running my life, that They were preventing me from being myself. I decided I had to get away and Jan and I flew to Majorca for a week in

January. I said in a newspaper article just before we left that if there was no let-up I would have to call it a day.

Life was fairly quiet for two weeks. Then the letters began to pour in again. 'We know you are very busy, *but . . .*' And I still felt that I was letting people down when I had to refuse their invitations because I was already booked. I read nearly all the letters I was sent and I always read the children's letters. I loved them for their straightforwardness:

'Dear Barry, I think you are very good, but Dai Watkins was much better. Can I have your autograph, please.'

It began to worry me that the adulation was alienating me from the human race. In a crowd at the National Eisteddfod I was talking to people when I heard a mother tell her small son to touch my hand. Well, I suppose that is a compliment, but I am not a god or a prince or a healer, but a man. Once, in Swansea, I was visiting a hospital and, to my embarrassment, a woman curtsied to me. In Rhyl a girl approached and, as I was saying beneath my breath, 'Don't do it, don't embarrass me,' she, too, curtsied. The people around me thought that was a great gesture and they laughed with pleasure, but it was to me another indication of the way I was being drawn away from people and reality.

Living in a kind of goldfish bowl is not living at all. I went to see George Best a few times and I quickly grew to understand his outlook and to have tremendous sympathy for him. People were pulling up outside his house to point at it and to photograph it; many times I have heard cars stop outside my house, wait a minute or two with the engine running and then drive slowly away.

Mrs. John with her children, Barry, Clive, Allan and Madora

The Cefneithen cricket team, Barry John second from the left in the back row

The Porthyrhy soccer team, Barry John third from right in the back row

George could at least escape by going to work at the football stadium; when I went to work I had to meet a lot of people and face the endless questions.

One aspect of the goldfish life was that I could rarely have a meal in peace when I went out to a restaurant. I quickly stopped booking a table in my own name because I became certain that one or two restaurant managers told their friends that I would be eating in their establishments at a particular time. As a result, people would be there at nearby tables and would have with them, as if by chance, a camera.

'Would you mind, Barry? Just for a second?'

And I would look up from my meal and smile and be blinded by the flash. And even quite late at night there would sometimes be sleepy-eyed children, brought out for a supper and a stare, by their parents. 'Would you mind signing your autograph, Barry?'

Of course, there were advantages: the best steaks, excellent service and all the trimmings.

As I ate my dinner I could often hear what people were saying:

'He's not very big, is he?'

'I thought his hair was darker than that.'

'That's his wife, then.'

At such times, and elsewhere, I had an almost overwhelming urge to do something shocking, like picking my teeth with a fork or slurping over a juicy bone. And on other occasions when people were being over-effusive I longed to be able to draw a whisky bottle from my hip pocket and take a swallow. It was just that some people believed I was some kind of angel. But I did not want to be an angel. I wanted to be a person with weaknesses like everyone else. I felt I could not tolerate this kind of existence much longer. Occasionally I had the curious sensation of not being in my own body, of looking at it as if it were some kind of robot. I was Barry John the rugby star and machine; the real Barry John had stepped outside for a while. In the year up to my retirement from the game I saw my doctor more times than in all the other years of my life put together. And I got into the habit of having a few drinks late at night as a drug to get me off to sleep.

The demands were unbearable. Leaving rugby had nothing to do with the game itself – the very thought of playing a match made my blood race just as it did when I was a schoolboy.

But family life had become impossible and, as an amateur player, I could not have continued leading this kind of life for many more months. I would have been doing no justice to myself, to my family, my firm, the Welsh team, or the devoted followers of Welsh rugby. In the end I would have let everyone down.

By the time of the Wales v. France match my resolve had hardened. I had decided that rugby should not be a total obsession, burning me out emotionally. It was a fulfilling and marvellous and large *part* of my life. But only a part. Yet to give it up was the hardest decision of all. Many times I wrestled with that insistent voice in the back of my mind which said: 'You were born to play rugby. Don't quit now.' It was the devil of a job to keep that voice quiet. I still hear it today from time to time.

2. Green and Gold

They gave my Uncle Lloyd an unforgettable funeral. So many people turned out that it should have been an all-ticket affair. The local policeman had to hold up the traffic as the great procession of people and cars passed through the streets of our village, Cefneithin. First, the coffin was taken to the chapel where people crammed in, sitting on the steps or wedging themselves in sevens and eights on benches where there was really only room for five. The singing went on and on for no one seemed to want it to stop. And at the cemetery people stood on graves to watch the burial. It was only to be expected, for Uncle Lloyd had made an impression wherever he went. He was never just a face in the crowd. He was always larger than life and his death was felt as a loss by everyone in our small community.

His laugh, his snort, his jolly and raucous shout, were known throughout the village, and in the neighbouring ones up and down the valley, in the meetings of the rugby club and on the terraces of Stradey Park, Llanelli's ground. His passage through the streets of the village was always slow, for as well as being gregarious and talkative, he was a bookie's runner, and his progress was punctuated by little knots of people, and laughter, and the passing of betting slips and cash.

He was a straightforward man and his language was ripe, but somehow his charm drained any offensiveness from it. He talked as it came, yet his swearing seemed to have a coating of honey, so that he could cuss away in front of the chapel minister, or the women, and they never batted an eyelid.

Often I went with him to the local rugby matches and witnessed his emotional involvement with the game. He was certain that young men who played rugby well had been blessed by the gods. Heavy rain never deterred him: he would get into his old green Morris Oxford – and he was an awful driver – and steer it to the touchline and sit there in the gathering fug, with the windscreen wipers going, his cap jammed upon his head and the oaths gently rolling.

If something happened on the field to upset him he would hurl his cap into a puddle – and with Uncle Lloyd in full spate you could almost see the ears of the mistake-makers burning.

Uncle Lloyd was a miner and had blue scars on his hands and dust in his lungs to show for it. When he came into our house he would sit for several minutes with his shoulders and diaphragm heaving, until he regained his breath. We youngsters knew that conversation was impossible then. We just had to wait until he had recovered.

I was sixteen when he became very ill. I remember that my mother sent me out to get some ice-cream for him – it was one of the few things he could manage to eat towards the end – and it was melting in the packet as I ran the half-mile to his house. When I reached his room downstairs I was shocked to see his condition. The cheerful and stentorian-voiced Uncle Lloyd I had known was now a little old man sunk into his bed, just a shadow. That visit had a profound effect on me and I felt a sharp sense of loss when he died shortly afterwards.

Coal mining and its effects were a large part of the background of my childhood. Our village was, and is still, typical of many in the coalfield of South Wales. My father, William John, worked for twenty-eight years in the Great Mountain colliery at the village of Tumble, a few miles from our home.

There were twenty-four houses in our street, a small and sympathetic community where we all knew each other, and very far removed from those impersonal modern estates. In twenty-one of the houses there were men involved in coal mining, so that at five o'clock in the morning there would be lights on and men getting ready to go on the early shift while their wives made their breakfasts and cut their sandwiches.

No one had much money. Every family was in the same boat more or less and we – and certainly our parents – knew what a shilling could buy. We were a family of six children and everyone in the street knew that we would feel the pinch if my father missed a shift. So if his alarm clock failed and my mother did not wake, he knew he could rely on the other men – seeing no lights in the house – to tap on the door or throw gravel at the window so that he could scramble out, eat his breakfast while he dressed, grab his green cap, muffler and hurriedly-cut sandwiches in his lunch box, and dash to the bus.

The dangers of working underground were rarely discussed, but even as a small boy I realised that awareness of the risks was always there, just beneath the surface.

If a siren wailed in the distance, the women, whatever they were doing – gossiping, shopping, or washing up – would stiffen slightly and we children were aware of a tension. It was the same when the bus from the pit was late in the afternoon. The women would talk quietly to each other to reassure themselves. The men understood all this very well. And if a miner decided to work some extra hours underground, and was therefore not on the bus from the pit, one of his workmates would go to his house to tell the wife and put her mind at rest before he himself went home for his tea.

My home village of Cefneithin lies in the valley of the River Gwendraeth in Carmarthenshire, about ten miles from Carmarthen, the county town. It has a population of eight hundred and is one of the little beads on a necklace of villages that runs down the valley. The names of the others, Pontyates, Tumble, Pontyberem, and so on, were impressed into my consciousness at an early age for, on the rugby field at least, they are rivals – and loyalty to your *bro*, your own neighbourhood, is a strong force, particularly in Wales.

Even today the first thing I turn to in the Sunday newspapers is not the reports and results of the big matches, but the corner of the *Sunday Express* that tells me how Cefneithin fared against the other teams in our district.

Only once did I defy the unwritten convention of loyalty to the village. My enthusiasm for playing rugby led me to turn out for my school one Saturday morning and then, thoughtlessly, to agree to play for Pontyberem in the afternoon. Well, the news got around – a Cefn' boy had played for the enemy – and the black looks and chilly

shoulders turned in my direction convinced me that I had
committed a considerable social offence. I never did it
again. But even today some people remember, and
remind me, of that boyhood error.

I was born in the early hours of the sixth of January
1945, at Low-land, a smallholding at Cefneithin, then
went to live at Voelgastell, which is about a mile from
Cefneithin. My parents were living there with my Uncle
Gwyn and Aunt Ethel. I was the second son. My brother
Delville is three years older than me, and I was followed
by Alan, who is a year younger, by Clive, three years
younger, Madora, seven years, and Diane, eleven years.
My mother, who was baptised Vimy, after the great battle
of the first world war, came from a large family herself:
she had nine brothers and sisters.

When I was two we moved to No. 14 Heol Tabernacl,
Cefneithin, a three-bedroomed semi-detached council
house with a small lawn in the front and a garden at the
back where my mother grew vegetables. This house was
my home for the next twenty-two years – until I went off
to college and then married. It was here that I first kicked
and threw a ball and was fascinated by the way it bounced
around the grass and off the walls.

I wouldn't want to change a day of my childhood. As I
look back on it, I count myself fortunate to have been
raised in a large and happy, noisy and united family.

Our part of Carmarthenshire, rather more than it is
today, was a thoroughly Welsh-speaking part. Welsh was
our first language, the one we normally used at home and
in the village. Like most of the children I spoke little
English until I went to school at five; we were taught
mainly through Welsh, but being young and adaptable

we very quickly became bilingual and by seven or eight were switching without much trouble into and out of the two languages. Today, because of the kind of life I lead, and because I live in an anglicised part of Wales, I tend to use English more.

But Welsh is the language I slip into naturally with family and friends. I would not, for instance, carry on a conversation in English with my mother. If I should telephone home and forget to slip into Welsh so that, for instance, I absentmindedly say: 'Hallo, how are you?' instead of: '*Helo, sut rydych chi?*' she would say, in a puzzled voice: '*Beth sy'n bod arnoti?*' – 'What's the matter with you?'

The language is important to me because it is part and parcel of my Welshness, of my upbringing and my personality. It is also a fundamental part of Wales – and Wales is important to me. This is where my roots are and, frankly, I don't want to live anywhere else in the world. I am proud to count myself a Welshman and, although it may sound a small thing, I always put down 'Welsh' in the nationality column of hotel registers. I have only written 'British' in the register when I was with the British Lions touring parties, and I felt it right and natural to sink my own nationality, temporarily, in the greater entity and enterprise.

Of course, the number of people who speak Welsh is declining and this is something that concerns many Welsh-speakers. I share the concern and I can understand the anxiety that leads people to demonstrate about the language. For my part, I am not one of nature's placard-carrying protestors and marchers. But I shall ensure that all my children grow up to be fluent Welsh-speakers.

Welsh was not only the language of home, play and school when I was a boy, but also the chapel. Our heads always swivelled round if the minister broke into English for a while during the service, for the benefit of some English visitors. Our chapel was Independent – what in England is known as Congregationalist – and it played a large part in our childhood. The influence of the chapels has declined a great deal and I remember that, as a teenager, I began to drift away from chapel-going. But as I reflect on our well-regulated Sundays, the memories are mainly fond ones.

Our chapel was a large grey building with seats for six hundred. When we were children we went there for the Sunday morning services and for Sunday school. As we grew older we stopped going to Sunday school and went to the evening services. When the sermons were dull and the long words flowed over our heads, we used to pass the time by counting all the green hats or the blue hats of the women in the congregation, though when the sermons were of the fire-and-brimstone type, so that the Devil knew where he stood, we used to listen more attentively, occasionally admiring a particularly theatrical performance. As we grew up we followed the tradition and moved away from the front part of the gallery to take our places with the older boys and the men; and as our voices deepened we were able to play a bigger part in the singing.

Of all the memories I have of our chapel, the strongest are of the pleasure we derived from some of the hymns. There are marvellous tunes that make my skin tingle now as much as when I was a boy. There was a strong sense of community and when the organ music signalled us to open our throats and sing we felt we were embarking on a joint enterprise: to sing the hymn loudly and strongly and see it through to the end.

Many of the tunes provided a direct line to a Welshman's past. Sometimes, in a party at a clubhouse or in a hotel, I've seen Welshmen laughing and gossiping in groups – and, suddenly, they catch the strains of one of the great anthems, like the 'Sanctaidd', on a gramophone record or sung quietly by a few people in a corner of the room. You can almost see the shutters go up on their eyes as their minds drift back to the chapels where they spent so many Sunday hours.

Our chapel was not a place we went to just for religious services. It was also a social meeting place and the source of some entertainment. One of the important qualities it gave us was confidence: as young children at Sunday school we were encouraged to master our shyness and stand up in front of the others to say a small piece. It is something that has stood me in good stead. I was also in the *cor plant*, the children's choir, and in *Urdd Gobaith Cymru*, the Welsh youth movement. I spent many happy evenings at *Urdd* meetings – and I was able to show some of the appreciation I felt by captaining one of the teams in a charity rugby match at Cardiff Arms Park to mark the movement's golden jubilee in 1972. In fact this was my last public appearance on the rugby field.

Sometimes we tried to feign colds on Sunday mornings so that we could stay at home and bask as the house filled with the smell of cooking. But my mother was wise to our games and sent us on our way. When we reached the middle of our teens she no longer insisted that we went to chapel and let us make up our own minds about it; I still went fairly often when I was seventeen and eighteen because I enjoyed it.

My father regarded the weekend as his deserved reward and respite. He went to our local pub on Saturdays and there he picked out his racing fancies and placed his bets. If they lost he would return to the house at two o'clock; if they won he would come back at half past four; but I never once saw him even faintly the worse for drink.

My father had played rugby as a young man, but for him the game was merely a recreation and never an obsession. Although his boys were rugby-crazy he did not become really excited about the game. He would encourage us in a quiet sort of way and come to watch us play from time to time, but he was not the kind of man who bellowed instructions from the touchline. I believe his attitude to sport was important: he always tried to keep a steady sense of perspective and this rubbed off on me. Of course, he was very proud when we did well. I remember a day when I had to leave the house at dawn to travel down to Hampshire for a schoolboy rugby tour. As I closed the front door I heard the bedroom window open: Dad threw down two ten-shilling notes, gave a smile and the thumbs-up sign and closed the window.

Like most of the boys in the village I usually spent my Saturdays, morning and afternoon – and evening too in the summer – kicking a ball. Our house backed on to Cefneithin park and in fifteen long strides from our back door I was down the path, through the hedge and on that stretch of grass where we boys let off steam, wore ourselves into exhaustion, and lived out our fantasies by beating the world's best sportsmen almost every day of the week.

I always seemed to be kicking a ball. Or throwing one in the air and chasing after it. I was fascinated by the way a ball behaved when I kicked it, or deflected it with the side of my boot or bounced it off a wall. I spent scores of hours kicking a football or an old bald tennis ball against the back wall of our home. And if I wasn't in the back garden or the park I was out in the street where the street lamp did double duty as floodlight in the gathering gloom of autumn evenings and as a goal post. If I didn't have a ball I dribbled with a stone. And I couldn't spy a piece of waste paper, or a cigarette-end, or a piece of wood, without running up and aiming a kick at it – and hearing, in my imagination, the roar of an appreciative crowd.

When I was about eight my parents, with others in the neighbourhood, bought us all some kit for Christmas. We wriggled into it as quickly as we could and dashed into the park for a game. Unfortunately our mothers and fathers had bought us shirts of the same colour and the game was rather confused.

We played rugby or soccer, but soccer for preference because it was easier to organise and suited small boys better. But while soccer was the important game for us from the point of view of participation, rugby was the game that gripped our imaginations and filled our talk. The players of Cefneithin rugby team were our heroes and the fortunes of the side on a Saturday dominated the conversation for the following week. In just the same way as a Cefn' victory seemed to put a spring in our fathers' steps as they went off to work on Monday, so we felt a certain happiness as we buttoned up our school coats and laced the black boots we always wore. My mother always knew if Saturday tea was to be a noisy or a subdued meal just by glancing at our faces and the set of our shoulders as we came in from the rugby ground.

When we played soccer we called ourselves Pele or Charlton or some other big name. But when we played rugby we were Evans or Jones or Jenkins, the stars of our own village team – and I think that's a good indication of the kind of regard in which we held our local heroes.

We imagined ourselves playing in front of the local people, in front of our own mothers and fathers, aunts and uncles. And this is a large part of what rugby in Wales, and particularly in West Wales, is all about. It is rooted in the small communities. From the day I first watched my local team my target was the honour of running out in the green and gold jersey of Cefneithin.

It is the long-term club player who is the backbone of rugby. The men who train hard and make sacrifices to play for the local side in all conditions for ten years or more – and without the facilities enjoyed by players in major clubs – are the men who have my total respect. In my experience they are the most knowledgeable people in rugby.

As I grew older I began to realise slowly that I had a talent for playing rugby and soccer. In the impromptu games in the park I always scored most of the goals and when I had the ball at my feet I could beat the other boys eight or nine times out of ten. Sometimes they used to make me play in goal so that they could make an even game of it.

I had an ability to dodge and feint, to make my opponents go the wrong way, and I found that when they had possession I had a fairly good idea of the way they were going to move.

During my years at Cefneithin primary school the head-master was Mr W. J. Jones, who had been a Welsh international in the early nineteen-twenties; and in my last year one of the teachers was Mr Ray Williams, who was a Welsh wing threequarter and a team-mate of Carwyn James. I was lucky, then, to get a lot of skilled rugby teaching.

The local junior schools took part in the Gwendraeth valley seven-a-side tournament and I captained our team for the last season before I left the school. I was a skinny little scrum-half. We were beaten in the final the first year and won it the next year. Enthusiasm was so strong that, when heavy rain washed out our practice session on the day before the second final, the headmaster arranged for the entire school to have lunch early. Then the staff cleared all the tables out of the dining-room and we had our practice in there. Ray was a good coach: he did not bother over-much with technicalities. He concentrated on showing us how to enjoy our rugby.

Our parents were just as enthusiastic as the teachers and when we played at home, in the park, they would arrive with buckets and bags full of sawdust to mark out the pitch and they stuck canes in the ground for uprights.

Not only did I have encouragement at school. Living directly opposite our house, on the other side of Cefneithin park, was Carwyn James, who played fly-half for Llanelli, was capped twice for Wales, secured his reputation as a coach during the British Lions tour of New Zealand, and had a great influence on me.

Whenever he used to trot out on to the park to do some training he was soon surrounded by boys. I was nearly

always the first there. We used to run with him, pass to
him and kick to him.

At times we must have been a nuisance but he never
asked us to go away. Carwyn is a patient man, and no
doubt he recalled his own boyhood when he watched
Cefneithin as often as he could and earned threepence a
game by retrieving the ball from back gardens on the east
touchline. After a while he used to take us to one side
and squat down and talk to us about rugby. He showed
me how to dummy, to side-step, the art he had learned
through watching the heroes of *his* youth, like Haydn
Jones and Bleddyn Williams.

Carwyn never gave us too many tips to think about at
any one time. Some coaches try to cram in too much but
Carwyn has always taken it easily. I think it was he who
impressed upon me the importance of watching good
players in action and of watching them in a particular
way.

I made a point of going to Stradey Park as often as I
could to see Carwyn himself in action. The first time I kept
my eyes on him for the first ten minutes of the match: I
didn't follow the ball, I followed him, trying to keep up
with his thinking and see what he did when he was off the
ball. In the next match I covered a different ten-minute
period in the same way, so that after a number of matches
I knew his game very well, his defensive moves, his
counterplay. When you think about it, any one player
does not touch the ball much during a match; what he
does when he is not in possession is at least as important as
what he does when he has the ball. This is one of the short-
comings of television coverage – the camera follows the
ball and you can't see all the supporting play. So I would

advise any young player who wants to learn to adopt the watching method I used. In my own case the technique stood me in good stead. When I had matured I found I could watch an opponent for a very short time and get important clues about his style and approach and how he was likely to react in varying situations. When you regard rugby as being a kind of high-speed chess, as I do, it is vital to know how the pieces on both sides are likely to move.

I failed the 11-plus examination the first time I took it and went to Cross Hands senior centre for a year. There I passed the entrance examination and went to Gwendraeth grammar school at Drefach, four miles from Cefneithin.

The school is a mixed one and serves all of the valley. The language of education is largely English, although in my day the colloquial language of playground and corridor was Welsh. A master would teach you in English, but if he wanted to talk to you personally, or if he called out 'Be quiet!' or 'Sit down!' he usually used Welsh.

The school was naturally rugby-conscious and I began to devote myself to the game. I looked forward to turning out in the school's blue and yellow hoops, and my chance soon came.

Asian 'flu struck down several members of the under-fifteen side one week and I was approached by John Hughes, the captain. John had a secret weapon: he had lost the top of his thumb in an accident and if he wanted your attention he would jab at you with the stump. He jabbed me in the chest one Friday:

'Make sure you're here tomorrow morning. You're in the team.'

That was my selection notification. I was elated. I was a

Barry John and Gareth Edwards on the sands at Port Talbot

Barry John with his wife, Jan

Roger Young shoots the ball out to Barry John during a team practise at the Newlands ground in Cape Town during the 1968 tour. Beyond John are Gerald Davies, Barry Bresnihan, Keith Savage and Tom Kiernan

small boy of twelve and here I was – picked for the admired under-fifteens.

The match was at Pembroke, against Pembroke grammar school. Our first fifteen was also playing there that day, so we all travelled down in the same coach. I felt very small indeed, twelve years old, only just out of the lollipop stage, sitting in the same bus as the mighty eighteen-year-old men of the first team, with their big talk and their loud laughter about things I didn't really understand.

I played at scrum-half, alongside my cousin, Ray Evans, who was fly-half. I was a skinny lad of less than seven and a half stones and many of the boys in our team, and particularly in Pembroke's team, seemed very beefy to me. I don't remember whether we won or lost; my lasting memory is of a hard match and many bumps and bruises. At half-time I was taken off the field, injured.

In my first year at the grammar school I played in the under-fifteens, the under-fourteens and the under-thirteens. With regular games periods and matches I was taking rugby kit to school about four days a week. And that still wasn't enough. When the school bus arrived in Cefneithin I was off it before the wheels had stopped turning, through the house casting off my school clothes and shoes, and out of the back door in casual clothes and on to the park grass, punting a ball high into the air – all, it seemed to me, in one fluid movement.

All the time, of course, I was building up a store of rugby knowledge.

At the age of fourteen I was selected for the Mynydd Mawr rugby team. Mynydd Mawr is Welsh for 'great mountain' and it is the name of our locality. The team was chosen from the group of schools in this area, among them

Gwendraeth, Pontyberem, Cross Hands and Tumble. It was a team of senior boys and I was one of the youngest chosen.

I was playing well enough for my friends to say that I must be in the running for an international cap. And, to be honest, I thought so, too. So I was more than pleased when I was invited to play in a trial at Carmarthen, and happy enough when the trial ended. There was heavy rain and the ball was slippery, but I felt that I had done enough to justify selection.

I knew that the team would be selected during discussions after the trial and that I would be informed on Monday. But I could not bear to wait that long. I knew I would not sleep. So I walked a mile and a half to the home of one of the schoolmasters in Cross Hands for I knew that he would know the composition of the side.

He opened the door at my knock and at once I knew by his expression that I had not been picked. He was disappointed. 'I'm afraid that you've been chosen as reserve, Barry.' The mile and a half back home was the longest walk of my life. I felt crushed and close to tears.

A few months later I was reserve in the final Welsh schoolboys trial at Llanelli, as I had been in the two previous trials. I did not get into the team. I abandoned all hopes of getting representative honours for a time; I felt that stupid men had kept me from what I had worked for and earned. I believe that other boys have been passed over like this and have been lost to Welsh rugby – and I remember that in the trough of my own disappointment I felt I would give up rugby and play soccer. But eventually my anger made me clench my fists and swear: 'I'll show them!'

By the time I was sixteen it was quite clear that I was

never going to be one of rugby's heavyweights, that I would be the ideal half-back build. I now began to play regularly at fly-half, which suited me better, and at seventeen I achieved the ambition I had nursed for years: I began to play in Cefneithin's green and gold.

In fact, all of the John brothers, all four of us, played for Cefneithin. Del, the eldest, was a wing forward in his early days and became a hooker, and he captained the club for two seasons. His playing days, though, came to an end when he lost the sight of an eye while he was working at his fitter's job.

Alan played for Cefn', for Llanelli, and went on tour with the Welsh team to Argentina. There is only a year between Alan and me and – you know how it can be with brothers – we were great rivals and had a regular cat and dog relationship. In our knockabout matches in the recreation ground we always played on opposite sides, otherwise there would have been a game-within-a-game as we each tried to outdo the other. Once, when we were both playing for Llanelli, Alan was hurt and I signalled to the trainer. Alan said he was all right and did not need help. I said he did. He said he didn't. There was a first-class brotherly row in the middle of the pitch.

Clive, at his peak, was a genuinely international class player, a wing forward with a rugby brain, the courage to match his ability, and, with it all, a rhythm. In one season with Llanelli youth side he scored a record forty-eight tries. Clive's misfortune – apart from injuries that have dogged him – was that he was a player several years ahead of his time and this was not recognised adequately. He was doing things as a wing forward, five years ago and more, that were considered unorthodox and were sometimes frowned on. He was using techniques that were thought to be the preserve of fly-halves and centres, in spite of his height and weight – over six feet and fourteen stone. Clive's approach is, today, the one that wing forwards are encouraged to adopt. He was very much a forerunner. He was a Welsh 'B' international and, but for his knee injury, would surely have become a full international. He played for Llanelli against the South African tourists in 1970 – that tough, marvellous match that the Springboks won by ten points to nine. Afterwards the Springboks told me how much they admired his performance.

In our district, as in others, there was a tremendous rugby rivalry between the villages. Cefneithin, Tumble, Pontyberem, Burry Port, Llandybie, Penygroes and Ammanford were at daggers-drawn on the field. Down in the pits the men from the villages worked together, helped each other, shared everything. But when it came to the lunchtime discussions and the talks turned to rugby, they divided into their separate loyalties. You were a Cefn' boy or a Tumble boy or a Pontyberem boy and it was stamped through you like lettering through a stick of rock. Hence the enormity of my breaking the unwritten code when, as a schoolboy, I agreed to turn out for Pontyberem against Resolven one afternoon.

Of course it was sheer enthusiasm that got me into trouble. I jumped at any chance to play rugby: I was in demand and enjoying myself.

When I was eighteen and in my last year at the grammar school I was asked to play for Carmarthenshire police force. I was thrilled – but I had to play truant to do it. It was all arranged by Hubert Peel, who was Llanelli's trainer and helped to run the police team. I agreed to play, but the main difficulty was that the match was to be on a Wednesday afternoon and I would be in school. Fortunately Wednesday afternoon was my games afternoon and I arranged to be on the fields, jogging around on a training run. Hubert agreed to be at the back entrance of the school with the getaway car. And, at the pre-arranged time, he gave a low whistle. I jogged out of the school and into his old black Wolseley which departed in a cloud of smoke for the match.

The police were playing Laugharne and my brother Del, a more experienced player than me, had warned: 'Stay at home, Barry, it'll be damned rough.' He was right. I needed all my skill as an artful dodger. Soon after the match started I fielded the ball and called out 'Mark!' – only to see the Laugharne full-back bearing down on me like a train and clearly unstoppable. No time to dodge. I raised my foot in self-defence and he collapsed like a shot stag.

Hubert Peel's Wednesday taxi service worked beautifully on two more occasions and, in all, I played for the police about half a dozen times. I scored a lot of points but all of them under the cloak of a *nom-de-rugby*. Had my name appeared in the papers I would have been in trouble on two counts: I wasn't a member of the police force and on three occasions I was a truant. So when one of the officials submitted a report to the local newspaper one of the other players took the credit for the points I scored.

The police players were good company and thoughtful, too. After the matches the players and some of their supporters would collect a small sum of money among themselves to reimburse me for my expenses – plus a little pocket money. The man taking the hat round would whisper that the collection was for 'the Special Branch' and everyone knew what he meant.

Through playing for the police force I got my big break in rugby. I was playing for them one Saturday against Swansea police. It was a hard match and I felt that I shone – and unknown to me there were some officials from Llanelli rugby club watching. Now Llanelli is a great club and to play for it is something that many West Wales lads dream about. I didn't know it at the time, but I had been 'spotted'.

During that Christmas holiday I was earning some money by helping a local man clean up the paintwork and fittings in an old cinema at Cross Hands. When I returned home one day there was a letter for me. It was an invitation to play for Llanelli.

I felt myself grinning like a monkey. I was about to take the big step upwards, changing from local green and gold into Llanelli's scarlet. Next day there was a headline in the sports page of the newspaper: '*New boy John in Llanelli team.*'

I felt I could make the appropriate rude gesture towards those who had deprived me of a schoolboy cap. I was still at school and going to play for one of the world's great clubs. I felt elated. I embarked on such a bout of cheerful whistling that people about me began to wince.

3. The White Blob

I went to our local Co-op store to buy some new boots. They weren't the streamlined Continental type, but the solid, old-fashioned flat-toed ones, and they cost me or, rather, my mother, thirty shillings.

On the morning of my first match for Llanelli my mother got me up early and when I came down to breakfast she was sitting in the kitchen polishing the new boots She looked pleased. Coming from a rugby family she knew what a big day this was. It was only half past six when I left to catch the bus down to Llanelli, to meet the rest of the team and board the train to Birmingham, where we were to play Moseley.

Snow was falling thickly when we arrived in the Midlands and I felt very glum as I watched it from the steamy window of the train. I thought the match would be called off. I felt elated when the word was passed round: 'It's on, boys.'

Llanelli had just played the 1962–3 All Blacks and for this match were not up to their usual strength. Moseley were too good for us and we lost by six points to five. Nevertheless I had a good début. I scored our five points in the second half by getting through a gap inside Moseley's fly-half and streaking up field. When I was clear of the grabbing hands only Mike Gavins, the

England full-back, stood between me and a try. As he bore down I side-stepped instinctively and touched down to the left of the posts. Marlston Morgan, Llanelli's skipper, breathed: 'Well done, take the kick' as he jogged past, and it was an easy conversion. In a curious way I felt a little embarrassed by it all. Scoring like that in my first match seemed a little imprudent – like making a maiden speech within two minutes of entering the House of Commons, and it was so very easy.

That match was played in my Christmas holiday and when the new school term started Llanelli wanted me to play against Neath, one of the big teams of Wales. But the school refused permission. Consequently I did not play again for Llanelli until the Easter holiday. This time I played for the first time at home, among my own people, at Stradey Park. It was the beginning of three wonderful years of playing for Llanelli, years in which I was able to study first-class players at close quarters, to build up my knowledge, to perfect my own game and to make numerous friendships.

Indeed, I believe I changed a good deal during my time with the club. As a teenager I was very shy but as a Llanelli player I came into contact with many people and travelled a lot. I well remember the occasion I first went to London with Llanelli – to play the Harlequins. I went to see my grandmother, Mam Low, to tell her that I was off to London and that I would not be able to do my regular Saturday morning chore – that is, to break up a week's supply of coal for her from the big lumps in the coal store. She could hardly believe that I was going to London. She had never been more than twenty-five miles from Cefneithin in her life and London to her was a big and bad place that she read about. So she gave me a little lecture about the pitfalls and the twisted values of the great city. Then she said she hoped we would win and, as I was leaving, she reached for her bag and pushed a crumpled pound note into my hand . . . just in case I got into difficulties in that far-off and unknown danger-spot.

Llanelli is the largest town and the industrial centre of Carmarthenshire. It is known everywhere for its tinplate and its rugby football, and for the Welsh song that Llanelli supporters roar out to urge their team on, 'Sospan Fach', which is a bit of nonsense about a saucepan boiling over. I can assure you that it is only properly sung in Llanelli!

I loved every minute of the time I spent at Stradey Park. The rugby here is played and talked about and lived with an intensity not found in any other part of the world.

In rugby terms Llanelli is the focal point for all the small villages of Carmarthenshire. They are the nursery clubs and they expect that their best players will go to Llanelli – and Llanelli expects to get them. There is no resentment at all about this. Well, not much anyway. And Llanelli recognises its debt by playing mid-week matches against the villages which draw large crowds and thus benefit the clubs. These are not, however, mere show games: the village side take a delight in trying to be giant-killers and always aim to give Llanelli a kick in the pants.

In the valleys of South Wales, and especially in West Wales, rugby is in the blood, to the extent that young men don't have to be taught side-stepping, feints, drop-shoulders and the refinements of the game. They are natural eels. In their story-telling, in recalling famous

57

matches, they can act out the swerves, feints and dummies as if recalling steps in a dance. There are plenty of fine players – but a lot of them have the sense to work at a career and keep rugby in its place. They are content to be local heroes and to abide by the golden rule: if you have talent you must play. If you are not wanted for Llanelli's match, you are expected to turn out for the village. Your talent belongs to the community.

At the same time as I was starting off on my playing career with Llanelli I became deeply involved with soccer, to the extent that I eventually had to make a choice between rugby and soccer.

It was while I was in my last year at school that two lads from Porthyrhyd, the best soccer club in our district, asked me to make up the team one Saturday. I did – and scored eight goals. Soon afterwards I signed forms to play in the local league. Frankly I did not know much about soccer tactics at that time and I remember asking Ryland Morgan, the centre-forward, what rôle I should play as an inside-forward. 'Stay five yards from me and you'll be all right,' he said. I'm afraid I followed his advice literally and after a while he turned round and begged: 'Stop following me around. You're getting on my nerves!'

I got into a routine of playing rugby for the school in the mornings and soccer in the afternoons. I scored a lot of goals and I was told that scouts from Coventry and Leeds were interested in me. I thought I might make the switch to soccer. But at the back of my mind was the feeling that I would miss the rugby world. After soccer matches I would scurry off to Cefneithin to join in the fun and gossip that followed the rugby, but I felt out of it because I had not seen the match. Soccer does not have the same sort of after-match social life.

And then Llanelli offered me a place in a club party going off to tour Germany for fifteen days. I could not go because I had A-level examinations, but I was thrilled that I had been asked. Along with my feelings about the warmth of rugby, that offer from Llanelli made me make the final decision. My flirtation with soccer was over and I moved, wholeheartedly, to rugby.

On the Saturdays when I was playing at Stradey, Dai Lewis, the local ironmonger and a dedicated rugby supporter, would come to my house in his car to take me to the ground. The other seats would always be occupied: in those days, as now, you didn't have empty seats when you drove to Stradey. I always had a tingling feeling of anticipation as we went through Felinfoel and then down the hill to Llanelli. I know Llanelli hardly at all. I only know the road to Stradey. It is an impressive stadium; it stands away from other buildings and has something of the air of a bull ring.

And inside the atmosphere is distinctive. Behind the scenes there is the friendliness that typifies Llanelli. In my day there was the president of the club, John Thomas, known as Johnny Millions because he was rich; Tiss, the baggage man, with the cheerful smile; Glan, the trainer, a diminutive fitness fanatic in a black beret, who was off from the touchline like a hare from starting blocks when a Llanelli player was felled, occasionally massaging the wrong leg, or sponging the wrong ear, in his enthusiasm; he was a vegetarian who always ordered steak at dinner so that he could pass it on to a particularly hungry player. There were the wives who came in to do the cooking for the meal after the match. A lot of supporters involved themselves with the club – and a place on the supporters club committee was coveted.

Llanelli has traditions going back to the very beginnings of the club more than a century ago. People talk in intimate terms of great players of the past as if they have only just hung up their boots. When someone talked of 'Albert' you knew he meant Albert Jenkins, a star of the nineteen-twenties who was reputed to drink six pints of beer before a match.

Of course there have been changes, but the old Llanelli is still there. The crowd is very Welsh: the songs and the shouts and the swearing and the comic-cuts are all in Welsh. Even if you had a bad game at Stradey you still had an enjoyable afternoon. Stradey was always something to savour.

This exuberant Welshness can, in fact, be exported. The Cardiff club love their fixture with Llanelli because Llanelli's supporters bring their special atmosphere with them. They are the Welsh Welsh; the Cardiff people are the English Welsh. The difference is not easy to put into words but it gives flavour to rugby, as it gives flavour to life in Wales.

At the end of the summer term, 1964, I left Gwendraeth grammar school. I was eighteen and I had made up my mind to be a teacher, preferably a sports master. I was accepted for a three-year teaching diploma course at Trinity College, Carmarthen, studying physical education, junior science and – rather strangely it may seem – horticulture: I had been told that this was easy and I believed I would be able to spend more time in the open.

During my first year at college I lived at home, but I was ten miles from Carmarthen and depended on buses and lifts. Like most young men I wanted a sense of independence, or at least an illusion of it, and I wanted to get away from home for a while. I found digs at Johnstown, about a mile west of Carmarthen, with Mr and Mrs Brian Davies. They had two boys, Andrew and Lynn. They all made me welcome – and one of the family – from the moment I stepped in the door and I lived there for a year. For my third year at college, however, I wanted to sample another experience and I went to live in the college itself. I moved into Room 3C in Tower block, furnished simply with bed, wardrobe, chest, table and chair. My years at college were among the happiest of my life: I had companionship, fun, enjoyable work, plenty of rugby and physical exercise, some pints of bitter here and there, and untroubled sleep.

Almost every week in the season I was playing for Llanelli and building up a reputation. Wales has a way of producing great outside-halves – Cliff Jones, Billy Cleaver, Cliff Morgan and David Watkins would spring to the minds of most Welsh rugby followers – and when I day-dreamed I imagined myself in their ranks. I was appearing quite regularly in the headlines and this was more fuel for the day-dreams and for ambition:

'A bright future is in store for this intelligent fly-half.' 'Barry John's craft turns the tables.' 'Llanelli inspired by their Scarlet Pimpernel.' 'Wonder Boy John.' And in 1965 a newspaper sub-editor coined the expression 'King John'. My team-mates and fellow students ribbed me. I was tickled. Who wouldn't be?

As the months went by and my confidence and ability

grew, the day-dreams began to have a serious edge to them: I reckoned there was a distinct possibility of getting into the Welsh side within a year or two.

Bleddyn Williams wrote in *The People*: 'A new fly-half star has been born in Wales. . . . He reminds me of Willy Davies of Swansea, whose acceleration through the gap made him a joy to play with and most difficult to mark.'

The player who had made the fly-half position indisputably his own at that time was David Watkins. But commentators were beginning to compare our styles and talk seriously of Barry John challenging Dai Watkins for his place.

'It must be Watkins-John fly-half duel,' one of the papers said before a trial match.

You can imagine that when I read this kind of speculation I felt the red jersey of Wales was within my reach.

I played in the trials of 1965–6 and was asked to be reserve for four international matches. Now I believed I was within striking distance, the recognised understudy. I looked forward to the following season, through the summer months, with a mixture of impatience, determination and, frankly, ambition.

In my last year at Trinity College I plunged into examination studies and embarked on my last season with the Llanelli club. Academically and physically I felt in good form. And to add to it there was a rather special kind of good fortune for me that autumn. I went to a Hallowe'en party at the Black Horse pub in Carmarthen and, as I was sipping a pint, I caught sight of a pair of frank dark eyes looking at me from the other bar. I looked. The girl smiled. I smiled back.

A friend caught sight of our exchanged glances.

'She's keen on you, Barry,' he said.

I felt rather keen on her. I inched away to arrange an accidental meeting. She was, I discovered, Janet Talfan Davies, the daughter of Mr Alun Talfan Davies, QC, a leading Welsh lawyer and, after six years at Cheltenham Ladies College she was at Trinity College studying to be an English teacher. I proposed a date and, subsequently, we began to go out together regularly.

Wales were to play the Australian touring side, in the first international of the season, on the third of December and I was asked to play for the Possibles against the Probables in the final trial at Maesteg. We won the trial by three points to nil and although I did a lot of accurate kicking and took my opportunities to run through the gaps – and showed up well enough against Dai Watkins – I felt at the end that I had had simply a fair game, not an outstanding one.

Still, I did not feel depressed; I had decided to be philosophical and wait for my chance to come. The following Wednesday the Australians played Newport, and drew three points all; when I read the match report in the next morning's *Western Mail*, and heard about it from people who had watched, I discovered that David Watkins – under the eyes of the Welsh selectors – had not had a good match. Apparently he had had a slow service and could not play the kind of game he liked. My view was that he was suffering from rugby fatigue. On the strength of what I read and heard that morning I crossed my fingers: the Welsh fifteen would be announced that night.

My friends felt, too, that I was now strongly in the running. We discussed it in low voices all afternoon, not daring to voice any hope explicitly, for fear of upsetting the gods of rugby.

In those days Bleddyn Williams presented a sports programme on BBC Wales television on Thursday evenings. And at ten-fifteen a crowd of us packed into the Welsh Room at the college; this was a common-room with easy-chairs, tables and, in the corner, a television set. We could expect the earliest news of the Welsh team on this programme.

Sure enough, Bleddyn Williams came on saying: 'Well, tonight we have the Welsh team to play the Australians. But, first of all, let's take a look at . . .' And to our agony he launched into another item of news.

I sat there, biting my lip, hunched down in my chair.

At last – the Welsh team. I was aware of the heavy breathing in the room. I could not hear what anyone was saying on the set. I concentrated my fast-misting gaze on the names as they were reeled up from the bottom of the screen. I knew that the scrum-half and the fly-half would be two names on their own and that if my name was there it would be short, just five letters: B. John.

And suddenly there it was. A short white blob. I couldn't read it through the pricking tears. But I knew I was in.

Propelled by some unimagined force I projected myself out of the chair and into the air. My own yell was overtaken by the yells of the tightly-packed group around me. In this great wild moment we all seemed to be several feet off the ground, a frenzied rugby tribe.

In that instant the television set gave a loud protesting bang, the picture collapsed to a vanishing dot and the sound was guillotined. So I did not know until the following day the composition of the rest of the team.

John being helped from the field after his disastrous injury in the match against Western Province at Cape Town

Barry John scores for Cardiff against St. Lukes

John puts through a short kick. John Slattery, Ray McLoughlin, and Peter Dixon follow up. Against Waikato, May 29, 1971

On winged feet I ran from the room pursued by the gang. We ran out of the building and shouted at the stars. We felt a deep need for a drink. But the college rules stated that we had to be in our rooms by eleven o'clock. I knew that Cefneithin would be in uproar. I wanted to be there and the group wanted to be there with me.

In this mood of euphoria we marched off to see Mr Cummings, the lecturer in charge of the hostel. One of my friends, Peter Davies, explained what had happened. But Mr Cummings, in this rugby-conscious college, in this rugby-conscious part of the world, knew little of rugby: he seemed unable to grasp what all the excitement was about.

Only three men, Peter said, had been picked for Wales while a student at Trinity: Ronnie Boone, Dewi Bebb – and now Barry John. He said firmly: 'Mr Cummings, this is the most fantastic thing that can happen to a young Welshman. *We have to go out.*'

Into these last five words he packed history, a whole rugby tradition, national pride, emotion and a hint of menace, so that Mr Cummings could see we were in deadly earnest. He understood and gave permission with a smile.

It seemed that within seconds we were in Cefneithin village. There was, if I may understate, a celebration.

Next morning we faced Mr Cummings again. He was taking us for a philosophy lecture. After a few minutes a student came in with a message. Mr Cummings took it and read it and then looked around.

'Is Mr John present?' I raised my arm.

'The principal sends his sincere congratulations on your selection . . . and, er, so do I.' There was a round of applause.

That was the only lecture I attended that day. I was too

excited to concentrate – and there were telephone calls from friends and journalists.

Then I was called to the college office to attend to a pile of telegrams. I went over and dipped into the small stack. By curious chance, the first one I picked up and opened said simply:

'MANY CONGRATULATIONS. DAVID WATKINS.'

4. Cap and Gown

You know how it is when you look forward to something so keenly that you start urging the time to fly by. I found myself looking at my watch and saying that at this time, ten, eight, five days hence, I would be setting off to play for Wales, tying my bootlaces in the dressing room, running out on to the pitch at Cardiff Arms Park.

I began calculating the number of breakfasts, lunches and hours to the third of December and willing the viruses that cause colds, influenza and sore throats to stay away from my door. On the Saturday after my selection I followed the usual procedure and did not turn out for Llanelli (for fear of getting an injury that would cost me my cap) and a friend drove me over to Llandovery where Llandovery College were playing Brecon. The college side was coached by Carwyn James and scored five tries in a beautiful match. I felt really inspired by it.

The following week I went to the university sports ground in Cardiff to meet and train with the other Welsh players and, most important of all, to get a working relationship with Alan Lewis, the Abertillery and Wales scrum-half. We had played together only twice before, the last time being in the trial at Maesteg. We practised in driving rain and I was disappointed because, with the ball

like a slippery herring, I had some trouble getting hold of
Alan's passes.

I joined the rest of the team at the Angel Hotel in Cardiff and, on the morning of the match, I was awake just
after six. Then I did a silly thing: I was wide awake and
wondering how to fill in the time, so I had a long hot bath.
This made me feel relaxed and tired and I learned later
that experienced players do not bath after their shower
on the Thursday night before the match. I found, too, that
it was better to go out on to the field with a slightly
unwashed and scruffy feeling.

After my soak I watched the early lorries rumbling by
and thought about the Welsh team. I realised that I did
not know all of them and I felt new and selfconscious.
Modern squad training has ensured that team members
get to know each other, that there is no longer any question of teams consisting of an established 'élite' plus new
boys. Later in my career I always remembered how I had
felt as a new cap and made a point of talking to newcomers and breaking the ice.

A large contingent of Australians were in Cardiff for
the big match, 'Waltzing Matilda' floated on the air and
Australian accents mixed with Welsh ones in the scrum of
bodies and gins and tonics in the bar of the Angel.

This was the fifth Wallabies touring side and the players
were out to do what none of their predecessors had done:
beat Wales. The reckoning among the sports writers and
most of the rugby public was that their chances were slim.

I was slightly nervous throughout the pre-match preliminaries, but I felt much better in the dressing room
when my red jersey was handed over and there were
handshakes.

In those days the old dressing rooms at Cardiff Arms Park were still in use. They had ancient and patched matting, benches pockmarked by countless studded feet – and bent nails as well as hooks on the walls. We players had to run out of the dressing rooms and along a corridor where there were some rather dangerous steps. An official was posted to call out: 'Mind the steps now, boys!' as we teetered by on our studs. You could have broken your leg on your way to your first cap. Then we had to run around the stadium and skip carefully over the television cables. And at last there were just two steps to ascend – and we were on the pitch.

I can never forget the moment I reached the turf for the first time in the Welsh jersey. It was everything – and more – that I had dreamed of. I breathed in the cold air and looked around at the fifty thousand faces in the crowd. It was an emotional moment. The butterflies inside were stilled by the kick-off whistle. It was time to think hard and get the measure of my opponents.

I did not touch the ball for four or five minutes; then it came out of a scrum and I took it away and swerved through a gap, passing it on as the Aussies moved in on me like a mobile wall. They played well. It was an open and fast game and we wasted some important chances. The Aussies deserved to beat us by fourteen points to eleven.

As we went off at the end I felt that I had played fairly well. I hadn't played a blinder by any means, but I hadn't made a lot of mistakes. I had not had the measure of Alan's passes and some critics blamed me for standing too far off. But Cliff Morgan wrote in his report: 'Barry John had a grand first international and looked as if he could beat the defence any time he chose.' It was heartening.

I was picked to play in the trial for the next international, against Scotland, and the scrum-half in the
Probables was Gareth Edwards, a student at Cardiff
college of education, and a Cardiff player. I did not know
him personally, although I knew of his growing reputation
as a determined and very talented scrum-half.

The trial was to be at Swansea and Gareth telephoned
me and suggested that we get together beforehand for a
work-out. I thought that a good idea and agreed to meet
him in Johnstown, near Carmarthen.

So, at half past ten on a bleak January Sunday morning,
Gareth was there. He looked fit and alert, handsome and
eager, in his smart track suit and clean boots. I, on the
other hand, was feeling scruffy and bleary-eyed and a
little aged through staying up too late the night before. My
kit was rumpled and plimsolls muddy.

The rain was pelting down as we jogged out to Ystrad
playing fields at Johnstown. Gareth's stride was bouncy
and he looked as if he was powered by a strong steel spring
as he moved about, darting, diving and sprinting. In
contrast I kept slipping on the saturated turf because my
plimsolls would not grip and my kit became muddier.

Gareth threw some passes at me and after a few minutes
I could see that we would get along well. We had the same
outlook on rugby, both spoke Welsh, and our personalities
complemented. Once this realisation dawned on me there
seemed to be little point in hanging about in the driving
rain.

With the rain running off my nose I said: 'Look, Gareth,
you throw them – I'll catch them. Let's leave it at that and
go home.'

He seemed a little irritated by this. It must have looked like laziness, which it was really.

'Don't worry about my passes,' he said. 'I can get them from anywhere. Just make sure you catch them, that's all.' Then he grinned: 'You're as confident and big-headed as I am.'

And that was the foundation of our friendship and our rugby 'special relationship' . . . although we didn't start playing together until the next season when we both began appearing regularly for Cardiff.

Gareth and I complement each other off the field and on it. I have a philosophical outlook and have always gone about things in a leisurely and quiet way if I could. Gareth is an explosion just waiting to happen. His temper is a bit on the hot side and he is a man of restless energy. Before a big match he is like a coiled spring. When we shared rooms he would pace about, throwing punches at me if I were in range, a tiger waiting to bound out of the cage. He would grab up a newspaper, read a few paragraphs, tear it up, hurl it down. If another player came in the room he would dive forward and wrestle with him.

He loves the battle of rugby. I would say that if he went twenty minutes in a match without body contact with an opponent he would have to collide deliberately with one of his own team. Just for a bit of action. He gives no quarter and his enthusiasm is almost tangible. That's one of the things that forwards like about Gareth.

In the dressing room, minutes before kick-off, he is moving up and down, smashing his fist into his palm, muttering: 'Let's get at them! Let's get stuck into them!', his body seemingly electrified and his eyes blazing.

If you are in Gareth's company you haven't a chance of

71

being bored. He is gregarious and a natural comedian and, on tour, the 'official' entertainer and organiser of the team's fun and evenings out. He is never on the edge of a crowd. If he sees a group of players chatting he elbows his way in and in seconds has everyone rocking with laughter. He's a willing clown, and therefore a great tourist, but he is also very sensitive about his own, or his team's, performance on the field. Defeat – in the time we played together – was a rare event and when it happened he would brood and re-live moments and analyse mistakes. He cares very deeply for Welsh rugby.

I was very lucky – it goes almost without saying – to have him as a partner. My game, after all, began at the end of his pass. Gareth has the perfect physique for a scrum-half; he's heavy for his height and his body has a low centre of gravity so that he is difficult to knock over. He is very strong, dedicated to physical fitness, fast and well balanced. His co-ordination is superb and he is a natural gymnast. He can leap like the salmon he loves to fish for and twist in mid-air. He is certainly the best scrum-half I ever played with and he, and scrum-halves like Chris Laidlaw, of New Zealand, and Dawie de Villiers, of South Africa are the best scrum-halves I have seen.

At one time his passing was not good, simply because he worried about it. But when he built up his confidence his action and timing became superb.

Our relationship was founded on our mutual respect and ability. That is stating the obvious, of course, but what made our half-back partnership important and extraordinary was our off-the-field friendship, our trust in each other – I knew he would make good passes, he knew I would catch them – and the Welsh language. This was the basis of the bond between us, partly because it was our native language and the one we always used when talking together, and partly because it was a secret code which we could use freely on the field to our great benefit – and our opponents' annoyance.

Our partnership – I liked it to be known as Edwards and John – was a natural and instinctive thing. We hardly ever talked tactics and our moves were spontaneous, not hatched in the dressing room or at a blackboard.

However modest the fixture we always played seriously. If we were way ahead we indulged in some fancy rugby to entertain the crowd. Some people have frowned on it, but I always regarded myself as an entertainer and when Gareth and I got up to some tricks on the field I always felt we were contributing to the game of rugby.

We never tried to outdo each other. If Gareth did not throw a pass to me I never felt resentment because I knew he was doing the instinctive, the best, thing in the particular situation. And if I were knocked down it was nearly always Gareth who was first there, looking down to see if I was all right.

There were many times when I felt that we were exploring new reaches of rugby in our partnership; this sensation fuelled our play. On a good many afternoons we ran out on to the pitch bubbling with enthusiasm. We felt like chefs who go into a kitchen and rub their hands and say: 'To hell with the lamb chops and spuds – let's make something really special!'

On the Saturday after my first damp meeting with Gareth we met at Swansea for the Welsh trial. It was a very tough game. As I was moving out of a scramble with the ball I swerved too hard, lost my footing in the mud and fell on another player as more men piled in. My right knee was badly gashed and I was helped from the field. David Watkins's uncle drove me to hospital in Swansea and the casualty officer sewed up the wound with eight stitches.

During the days that followed my knee was stiff and I was in pain when I walked. Only three days before the international I had to get around with the aid of a walking-stick. I should have withdrawn from the team. I was a fool not to. But I felt I could not give up my newly-won place. Pride, stupidity, and the glory of playing for Wales, kept me from telling the truth about my injury. I snipped out the stitches myself, before the wound was completely healed.

Gareth was not picked for the team. Billy Hallin, of Cardiff, was chosen as scrum-half and I was a little surprised because Bill and I were both individualists on the field, two of a kind. We clashed rather than complemented. Moreover, I was used to the long passes I had been getting at Llanelli from Gareth Thomas and Dennis Thomas, and Billy did not throw out long passes because they were not his style.

I did not play well at Murrayfield. I was painfully aware that my injury was slowing me down and I made a lot of mistakes. And technically I showed up poorly. Without the long passes I needed I had to change my approach. Billy and I just did not click together as half-backs. Wales lost by fourteen points to five.

I felt in a dark grey mood on the homeward journey and, back in Wales, I did not feel like going out much. I did not want to be seen; I felt a failure, a young man who had once shown promise and had let everyone down through his inadequacy.

The brooding lasted for days. And at last I faced the fact that my pride had swamped my common sense. I had not been fit at Murrayfield and you cannot play international rugby unless you are. It was a lesson. I did not expect to be picked for the next match, against Ireland, and I was ready for the disappointment when it came.

It came, in fact, the following Thursday week. Billy and I had been picked to play for the Barbarians. This is one of the honours of rugby. My father always said that to be asked to represent the Barbarians was an accolade, as important as being asked to play for your country or for the British Lions. I have played for the Barbarians six times and I have always considered that selection for the side is a mark of the regard in which a player is held in terms of his sportsmanship. A bad loser or a gloater-in-victory does not get picked, and bad-tempered flare-ups are rare in Barbarian games.

Anyway, as we were lacing our boots in the dressing room, Billy turned to me and said ruefully: 'We are going out on the field as the current Welsh half-backs. What will we be when we leave it?'

Later we learned that we had both been dropped from the Welsh team. I was chosen as reserve and remained reserve until the end of that season.

During the summer of 1967 Dai Watkins was tempted to the Rugby League club Salford, leaving the field clear for me. Although it seemed that I was the obvious fly-half choice for Wales I felt that there might be some genius waiting in the wings to grab the place. I made up my mind that there should be no complacency on my part.

Dai was a first-class player and had proved it. I felt that I had to do the same.

I left Trinity College at the end of the summer term of 1967 and I had already decided that I wanted a new course to my life. Months earlier I had told some of the officials of the Llanelli club that I would not be available to play when the season resumed in September and I suggested they might drop me occasionally to try out possible replacements.

Later I made my position clear by announcing that I had filled in a form applying to join the Cardiff club. Llanelli, however, decided to make one last effort to get me to stay. Four club officials drove to my home for a chat. They settled themselves in the parlour and the conversation was about the Llanelli club, its long history, its traditions and the loyalties it inspired in its players and the people who supported them at Stradey Park. The words tugged at my emotions.

But I was determined to go.

I explained what lay behind my decision. I was not unhappy with Llanelli and I admitted that I owed the club, and the officials and supporters, a great deal. Leaving Stradey would be a wrench. But rugby, I said, was only a part of my life and I wanted to keep it that way. Other players had allowed rugby to take over their lives and drain them emotionally. I wanted to avoid that. I wanted a change. I had lived all my life in West Wales and I wanted to do something different, to live in a different part of Wales, to sample life in the capital city. It may not be a long way in miles from Cardiff to Llanelli – but there is a difference.

My decision, I told the club representatives, really had little to do with rugby. At last they seemed satisfied, or at any rate they indicated that they understood and respected my wish to have a change of scene. There was no ill-feeling and they left in their limousine.

Some people in West Wales were critical when they heard of my move to Cardiff.

'You're just thinking about yourself,' someone told me, point blank.

'Yes,' I said, 'I am thinking about myself.'

It was whispered that I was going to Cardiff simply to join the Cardiff club and get into a brighter limelight in front of the Welsh selectors. That was nonsense of course. I had my first two Welsh caps when I was playing for Llanelli.

A change. That was what I wanted. Some people couldn't understand a simple human thing like restlessness.

Cardiff accepted my application and invited me to a trial. I played in the junior team in the trial; although I had already played twice for Wales I never expected that fact to give me a passport into the Cardiff side. I knew that I would have to prove myself in a trial.

My first match in Cardiff's blue and black was against Headingley on a wet afternoon in September and, although I felt I played adequately enough, I had the feeling that something was lacking in my game. It was a feeling I experienced in several other matches as the season wore on. I next played for Wales against the 1967 All Blacks – my first match with Gareth Edwards – and, in very muddy

77

conditions, I made the mistake of playing deep instead of going up to the New Zealanders and kicking and keeping pressure on their defence.

Meanwhile, I had become a schoolmaster. I had been appointed physical education teacher at Monkton House School in Cardiff, a private school for boys aged between eight and sixteen. I was also appointed to teach general science and English literature.

I got on well with the boys. I decided it would be a bad thing, psychologically, to show even a trace of unsureness while standing in front of the class. I aimed to be sympathetic and to inject some humour from time to time, to make the lessons more bearable if they couldn't interest everybody. I did not, however, maintain a monopoly of jokes: if a boy had a funny story or experience to relate I encouraged him to stand up and tell it to the rest of the class. This helped to break down shyness and encouraged confidence – as I had learned as a boy in chapel – and confidence is half the battle in education.

It was rather odd, at first, to hear myself called Sir, and it was odd, too, to realise that some of the boys I was teaching were somewhat richer than I was. My monthly salary was forty-eight pounds and I had to budget carefully. That was a new experience for I had been a student and had lived at home a lot and I have a happy-go-lucky attitude towards money.

I was reflecting on my lack of finances in a bus one day – I had just given my last, rock-bottom coppers to the conductor – when I observed a boy from my school ask for a ninepenny ticket and peel a note from a sheaf of fivers to pay for it.

At that time I was sharing a house in Cardiff with

Gerald Davies, Ken Evans, Malcolm Bulpitt and Garfield Jones, all West Walians, and we were having to fend for ourselves. Gerald Davies had invited me into the house on hearing of my homeless condition when I arrived in Cardiff. Gerald is a serious man, but his rare wit and sense of humour contributed a lot to the fun we had. I had played against him at school – he had been at Queen Elizabeth grammar school in Carmarthen; we had both played for Llanelli and we were united by the bruise of having been in the Llanelli team thrashed fifty points to eight by the Harlequins.

Some of the facilities at Monkton House school failed to impress me. The science laboratory seemed somewhat under-equipped. And when I arrived the only sporting equipment was an old football, and this had a hole in it.

The headmaster was the late Mr C. A. Williams. It became clear to me within a week or two of my joining his staff that our personalities clashed. I found him a little crusty. No doubt he regarded me as brash. He had well-tried methods of teaching and ideas about education backed by long experience. I was young and had different ideas.

At morning prayers one day his sharp eyes caught me stifling a yawn and he also noticed that I did not join in the singing of a hymn. He asked me not to attend morning prayers again. Later we had an argument over my method of teaching English. I believed I was being progressive and making the lessons enjoyable, but he did not approve. When I look back on my short teaching career I realise I could have been more diplomatic.

There was one subject, however, on which Mr Williams and I could talk amicably and at length. Rugby. He had a lot of knowledge about the game and took it very seriously. On one occasion I was talking to him about Cardiff Arms Park and I referred to it casually as 'the Park'.

He reprimanded me at once. 'It is not "the Park". It is Cardiff Arms Park.' It was a little pedantic of him, I suppose, but I respected him for his insistence on the full title.

I was in my second term at Monkton House when there was a lot of talk, in the rugby clubs, and in the newspapers, about the likely composition of the British Lions party to tour South Africa that summer, 1968. I was strongly in the running to be one of the outside-halves and when the subject came up in a conversation with Mr Williams he told me he hated South Africa's apartheid policy, and, although he loved rugby, he disapproved of a tour to South Africa.

Although I was a likely candidate for the tour my self-confidence at this time had diminished. I felt that I was not playing outstandingly, that I was only just doing my job and not much more. Gerald told me that he felt the same. It was a simple case of rugby fatigue.

We were looking after ourselves in our house, rather inexpertly. We were not feeding ourselves properly and we were turning up for training sessions with damp kit. We were eating and sleeping rugby, with club matches, trial matches, squad training. With all this, and our jobs, our lives were crammed and disordered.

I had no doubt about my ability on the field, but I began to doubt whether I could play a whole season of top-class rugby, and so I began to worry and my game to suffer: my timing faltered increasingly and that got me rattled and I started to do things in the wrong order. I

Alan McNaughton tackles Barry John in the first Test in New Zealand,
June 26, 1971

John on his way to scoring what was probably the most brilliant individual try of the whole 1971 tour, against New Zealand Universities at Wellington, July 6, 1971

found myself being grabbed from behind – and that should not happen to an international fly-half. I was caught up in a vicious spiral.

It was at this unhappy stage that, to my lasting gratitude, Ray Williams stepped in. Ray is the Welsh coaching organiser, the first man appointed by the Welsh Rugby Union in this professional capacity. He is not involved with the national team – he is the link between the Union, the schools and the county associations – but his opinions are highly valued at all levels of rugby in Wales and top players seek his advice. He has made, and continues to make, an enormous contribution to better rugby in Wales. Ray, of course, is a thinker and his deep insight into rugby is not restricted to tactics and technique. He understands players and the pressures on them and their human weaknesses. In discussions about the game he never dismisses someone else's ideas out of hand if he disagrees with them. He listens, discusses and points out alternatives. Conversations with him have certainly broadened my approach to rugby.

He also has the ability to see when a player is in trouble. 'Come out and have lunch with me,' he said one day.

We settled into a restaurant in Cardiff and I listened to him as he analysed my problem. He pointed out the reasons for my apparent lethargy and the lack of edge in my game. 'At the moment,' he said, 'you are in the running for the Lions tour, even though you haven't been showing up too well lately. But if you carry on like this you will be in trouble and you will be relying too much on other people.'

He told me to pull myself together, and then how I should go about it. First, he boosted my ego, praised and explained all my qualities and then mentioned other leading rugby players who had gone through bad patches. 'Don't try to impress,' he said. 'Don't be over-anxious. Don't hunt around frantically for gaps in the opposition. Just wait calmly for the openings to develop, and then take your opportunity. You'll find you will be playing your old game again and you'll soon have your confidence back.'

Ray gave me the reassurance I needed and put my problems into perspective. That was one of the most important lunches of my life. Ray's talk and gentle advice made me feel much better. What he did was surely an aspect of skilful coaching. Carwyn James is another man with the same thinking approach to rugby and to players' problems, and I have gone to him from time to time when I felt that I was not putting my game together properly.

On two occasions, to get away from the pressures of first-class rugby, I telephoned Cefneithin rugby club and asked them if they would put down A. N. Other for their next second fifteen match – and I would go home for a complete change and for a game of rugby that I regarded as a kind of therapy. It was important for me to play without the usual pressures of big rugby, but I always played seriously and never held back. I couldn't afford to: West Wales rugby is robust and you can't give less than one hundred per cent. I don't think that Cefneithin had hopes that an international player would make a world of difference. If they did they were mistaken. One day I turned out for Cefn' second fifteen against Llangennech. We lost – it was the team's first defeat of that season – and I missed four penalties!

People still remind me of that day – and of another day,

too. This was in 1964, before I became an international, when Cefneithin were playing in the West Wales cup competition against Pontardulais. The match was on New Year's Day. On the evening before, the team agreed to stick together: we planned to look after each other and make sure that no man had too much to drink. We behaved for a few hours in the dance hall at Pontyberem and it seemed that we would all go to our beds with clear heads. But disaster struck in the form of a bottle of whisky that we won in a raffle. We had a sip, then another, and another . . . and finally washed away our sin with some glasses of beer. The next day most of our side looked decidedly unhealthy. After a few minutes, though, we were awarded a penalty – a virtual gift of three points for the kick was to be taken fifteen yards out and directly in front of the posts. I took the kick – and missed. We lost by three points to nil and, that evening, the atmosphere in the club was wintry. I slunk out and was in bed by half past eight . . .

On the day the tour party for South Africa was announced I was on tenterhooks. I walked up and down outside the Cardiff rugby club office, killing time until noon when I knew the selections would come through. At last, at two minutes past twelve, I walked into the office. Ann Davies, the secretary there, was on the telephone taking down names. When she saw me she smiled and gave the thumbs-up sign. I knew I was in. And soon afterwards she put down the phone and said that six of us from the Cardiff club were in the tour party.

I went back to school after lunch and told the boys my

good news. I left the school at the end of term and, though I did not know it then, my teaching days were over.

Naturally everyone was delighted that six of the Cardiff players were going on the tour. There's a special magic about the name of Cardiff in rugby and rightly so. There is an atmosphere and a certain style about the club that, once sampled, makes you understand why players do not want to leave it. Llanelli is an equally great club – but in a different way. I count myself as most fortunate to have played for both. Cardiff makes a player feel that he is a somebody and every player is treated in the same fashion whether he is a famous international or a relative un-known. The trophy room at the club is a rugby museum, with photographs of teams going back to the last century, and when you discuss rugby here you are keenly aware of tradition . . . with all those eyes looking down on you from the photographs.

When I was with Cardiff I always looked forward to the matches against Llanelli. On two occasions I played against my brothers, Alan and Clive – they were the wing-forwards who had to mark me and there was, as I recall, a distinct absence of brotherly love! The Llanelli–Cardiff fixture is a sort of miniature international and I remember that in the last one I played in, at Cardiff Arms Park, I kicked the dropped goals that gave us victory at a time when it seemed Llanelli might have it all sewn up. Clive said at the end: 'Trust you, you so-and-so.' A Llanelli supporter swung his fist towards me as I left the field. I ducked. I heard later that in West Wales my name was mud that night . . . there's nothing quite like a little bit of needle to add zest to rugby.

5. Finger in my Collar

Just before joining the tour party I went home to Cefneithin. There was a small stack of letters waiting for me
on the mantelpiece. They were all short notes, mostly
anonymous, and most contained money.

'Absolutely delighted for you' – five pounds;

'Well done, Barry' – a pound;

'Have a drink on the boys' – ten pounds;

'Good luck' – a two-shilling postal order.

In one of the local pubs a bottle had been placed on the
bar counter and it had been filled with sixpences, florins
and coppers. A local group gave a concert and sent the
proceeds to my house.

I was very touched and grateful. That is one way the
amateur game works in Wales; I don't think the same
thing happens in England.

People in the rugby-oriented villages understand not
just the finer points of the game, but what a player gives
in return for being chosen for his country, how much the
honour can hit his pocket. They know his family and his
circumstances. And if they feel the need is there they take
the hat round.

A British Lion doesn't make a profit. And that is an
understatement. The tour organisers give him two blazers,
a navy blue one with a large badge on the pocket, and a

black one with a small and more discreet Lions badge, for evening wear. With these come one pair of grey trousers, a tie and bow-tie for dinners and receptions. The player supplies his own shoes and shirts but he gets his playing strip given and a voucher for a pair of boots. He provides his own training kit, but the 1971 Lions in New Zealand were given sharp scarlet track suits.

On the two Lions tours I took part in, to South Africa and New Zealand, I had a pocket money allowance of ten shillings a day. At the time of the South Africa tour, I was single and living from day to day, so I didn't worry much about the financial side of things. (When I went to New Zealand my salary was paid.) But many players in the past have turned down tour invitations because they knew they would lose earnings. Wives have gone without luxuries and holidays so that their men could go on three-and-a-half months' tours. Rugby wives are understanding in the main – they have to be – and so are those employers who gladly give leave of absence and keep jobs open. So there is no money in touring – and touring itself involves a lot of travelling and living out of a suitcase and absence from home. That's the negative side. There's a plus side, too: a rugby tour is a unique and an exciting experience and I count myself lucky to have been a Lion twice.

Before setting off for South Africa we spent a week at Eastbourne; getting to know each other and training together, under the eyes of David Brooks, the tour manager, and Ronnie Dawson, his assistant. After some days we became aware of a bond, of a developing team spirit. We ate and slept well and we felt we were professional sportsmen being groomed for the great adventure of a long rugby safari.

86

Just before we left Eastbourne an official from the South African embassy in London came down to give us a talk about his country. He finished by warning us that the tour could be wrecked if one of us did something foolish, like going to bed with a coloured girl. It was impressed upon us that such a transgression could cause an international incident.

'Don't,' he said, 'get dragged into political arguments about South Africa. Accept the South Africans' philosophy as it exists – and talk only about rugby.'

At that time I did not give the apartheid situation in South Africa very much thought. I didn't know much about it and it appeared to me to be a vague problem in a hot country far away. Had someone tried to persuade me not to go to South Africa, to make a dramatic gesture, I should probably have been impatient and asked what right he had to interfere with my dream adventure. But I was soon to learn more about the country and apartheid.

Our Boeing 707 landed at Jan Smuts Airport, Johannesburg on the thirteenth of May and we stepped out into the early morning, grinning and waving to the welcoming crowd and to the photographers. South Africans are sports-crazy people – they have plenty of opportunities for outdoor pursuits with their climate – and they were really looking forward to the tour.

I did not play in the first match, against Western Transvaal at Potchefstroom, and I was pleased to have time to get properly acclimatised. Many matches in South Africa are played on grounds between five thousand and seven thousand feet above sea level and it takes a while to get used to the altitude. I recall that my first high-level training session left me panting for breath.

Our next match was with Western Province, at Cape Town. Of all the South African provincial fixtures, the consistently toughest are Western Province and North Transvaal – they are the Llanelli and Cardiff of South Africa. I think we did well to win for it was a hard match and some of the boys took hard knocks.

The rough and tumble of rugby can be a big problem for tourists in South Africa because the grounds are usually harder than anywhere else where rugby is played – and the game is very fast, definitely fifteen-man rugby.

Rucking is not a strong feature of the game in South Africa because the ball changes direction so rapidly: you really have to have your wits about you. This tour was the last before the new kicking rule, the dispensation law, came in – and so there was a great deal of kicking, particularly high kicking.

With this kind of rugby, with the hard grounds and body collisions at high speed, casualties are inevitable. An especially painful injury is a grass burn, and to guard against it touring players are recommended to rub methylated spirit into vulnerable points like elbows, knees and hips, to harden the skin.

Beating Western Province was an important scalp for us and, off to this good start, we faced the next fixture, against South West Districts, with confidence. We played at Mossel Bay, a beautiful seaside ground, and I, for one, felt in peak condition.

I lost my head a little at first, running past man after man, and playing excitedly. I realised that I was not passing as much as I should and I resolved to discipline myself. I felt in this match that I could really enjoy my game, that from now on I was going to play some great rugby. I didn't have to battle and slither through thick mud, as I did at home; I was on top of the ground, light and nippy, swerving, feinting, dummying with ease, kicking beautifully. I felt invincible. I missed the next match, but in the one that followed, against Natal, at Durban, I again had this marvellous sensation of playing well.

The first Test was at Loftus Versfeld, in Pretoria, and when we walked out from the dressing room to look at the ground, we felt like ants. The vast grandstands seemed to us preposterously tall and therefore unsafe. It seemed that some giant scenery artist had pasted cardboard cut-out people high in the hard blue sky. The pitch, we noted, was hard and in the middle of it was a cricket square which was as hard as a slab of Welsh slate.

After about ten minutes we had a penalty on our own ten-yard line. Tom Kiernan, our full-back and captain, was, at first, going to slam the ball into touch, but he passed to me and I went straight through a gap, outside Jan Ellis, and veered towards the centre, with the South Africans swinging in on me fast. I had three men outside me and we were going well. A try seemed within our grasp. For a half-instant I thought I could pass out to my right. But it would have been a long pass. Too long. I dummied and bent under the grabbing hands and raced on for the try line. Only the full back to beat.

But I'd made a mistake. I had not anticipated Ellis's tremendous acceleration. His determination. I was aware of his shadow — my feet were in it — of his breath and pounding feet. Instinctively I accelerated — then suddenly slowed to throw him off.

It very nearly worked. But by cruel chance a finger of

his stretching hand caught under the collar of my shirt. It was enough to upset my balance.

I fell, tumbling over, on to my left shoulder and I felt the bone crack as I hit the ground.

I said to myself: 'Collar bone gone,' and lay there panting and cursing. An ambulance man came running over and I made sure he did not handle me without supporting the injury. I went off the field and into the cool dressing room. I took a pain-killer tablet. I had tears in my eyes.

I felt a wave of disappointment. I had found the place where I really wanted to play rugby; I had been like a pianist who finds a fine piano in an acoustically perfect room. Now I was on my way to hospital.

The doctor diagnosed a greenstick fracture – the kind that children suffer from because their bones are not mature – and after the X-ray I was strapped up, had my arm put in a sling, and went down to the reception desk. There was hardly anyone about on this bright, hot afternoon, for most people had gone to the match. I was still in my dirty playing kit. A porter came by and said that if I would wait a while he would drive me to the team's hotel. I accepted his offer and went to the hotel. That was almost deserted, too. I felt fed up and went up to my room. I felt alone and sorry for myself. Hearing that the Lions lost by twenty-five points to twenty did not make me feel better.

When the players returned to the hotel after the match Gareth came in to see me and cheer me up with his chat. And then J. B. G. Thomas, the *Western Mail*'s veteran rugby writer, came in to the room to see how I was. No doubt he saw at once that I was feeling down. After a few words of reassurance he said: 'Leave everything to me. If you want anything, it's on the *Western Mail*.'

That made me feel better. J.B.G. said he would write about my injury in his report and follow that up in the following days with short progress reports.

I expected to be told that I would have to fly home. That's the usual drill with an injured tourist. But because I had this curious greenstick fracture it seemed there was a chance it would mend and that I might be able to play in the last month of the tour. I was told to submit to a medical inspection so that the doctor could give an opinion and I was warned that I would have to perform some exercises to show how my injury was improving. Before I went in to the doctor I took my arm out of its sling and drank some whisky to deaden the pain of the exercises. I did the movements, stifling the winces, and the doctor seemed satisfied.

David Brooks, the manager, took an optimistic view. 'Even if you can't play for some time you will be able to start training when the crack has healed. In the meantime stay and enjoy seeing the country. We're going to the Kruger National Park in a few weeks – make the most of it.'

I felt happier after that, but I loathed being the odd man out in the party. In the mornings the boys would be up and about and eager to go off training. I watched them go with my morale at low tide. To spin out the mornings I used to have my breakfast in bed, as late as possible, and get up and dress myself very slowly. Then I joined them when they returned at lunchtime and got into the swing of things.

But still I couldn't help feeling a hanger-on. I felt my fitness waning and I began to doubt that my injury would heal in time. It didn't. And being on a rugby tour as a player who cannot play is hard to take.

In my spare time I used to visit children and old people in hospital, to chat about rugby. I rather enjoyed that because my visits gave pleasure and I got a lot of pleasure in return.

Being one of a group of honoured guests, I usually saw South Africa's best side, and it is a beautiful country, no question about that.

To someone coming from a country like ours South Africa is, physically, an exhilarating land. The grass and trees, all the vegetation, have a different texture. As a sportsman I was attracted to the outdoor life which is a large part of the way of living in South Africa. Many houses have built-in barbecues, there is a great emphasis on sport, and at four o'clock on Friday afternoons everyone – well, all the white people – seem intent on starting the weekend and enjoying themselves.

We were lucky enough to see many parts of South Africa. I loved Cape Town for its beauty and I enjoyed our safari in the Kruger National Park where we stayed in well-appointed 'huts' and got close to lions, elephants, giraffes and many other animals. During the tour some of the party went out hunting and shot a few deer. That never appealed to me personally for I could never bring myself to kill a wild animal for pleasure.

For all South Africa's many attractions, however, there is an unhappy side to life there from which you just cannot escape. The country's apartheid policy is like an extra ingredient in the atmosphere.

One day we were taken to see gold mines and of course, there were many black men working there. We saw a group of them loaded into a cattle truck – they weren't being treated like human beings at all and the sight sickened a lot of us. At rugby grounds the people are segregated and the black people are penned like cattle. The apparatus of apartheid, simple things like the signs saying Blacks Only, Whites Only, is disturbing to a newcomer. I don't know quite what I had expected to find and see in South Africa, but equality and classlessness are a part of my background and, naturally, I measured the things I saw against that. It is true that I was not in South Africa a long time, though I was there for three and a half months, and I was certainly in a special position. For that reason I have always avoided making hard judgments. Sometimes we had explanations made to us which gave an insight into the white people's outlook and which helped us to understand a little of a complex situation. It seemed to me, though, that a lot of black people in South Africa do not live; they survive.

We obeyed the rules and stuck to rugby in our conversations with people, but we found that many of them were curious to know what people outside thought about their country and its political and racial situation. It struck me that some of them were searching for some kind of reassurance in a situation in which they felt uncomfortable and a certain lack of confidence.

6. Lure of the North

When I returned to Wales I had a fine sun-tan and not much else; neither job nor money.

At first I felt entitled to be free for a week or two to get plenty of sleep, to adjust to ordinary life after the extraordinary existence of a rugby tourist and, frankly, to bask just a little in the reflected glory of having been a British Lion. It had, after all, been a great adventure.

Jan and I decided to go to North Wales in her little car for a short tour among the mountains and lakes. We had sixty pounds between us, but the trouble was that I could not make the adjustment to day-to-day living and still lived as a tourist, ordering whatever I fancied in hotels and restaurants and urging Jan to do the same. Within three days we were almost broke and had to come back home.

I had imagined that I would never have any difficulty in getting a job. People had always said to me that, as a Welsh international and British Lion, I would have doors opened for me and jobs would be available, as fruit in a dish. There were hands upon my shoulders and reassuring smiles: 'You'll be all right, Barry, bach.' I believed in this myth, so that after a few days I was concerned and surprised that there were no letters for me, no callers at the door offering me employment. It was two or three weeks before the realisation really penetrated that I should have to go out and find a job myself, like anyone else.

I was living at home in Cefneithin and I felt that people were whispering that I was the international who did not like work.

There was nothing in teaching available and I had not trained for anything else. I found it difficult to imagine myself doing a job outside the field of education. By the middle of September there was nothing in prospect and one morning I walked two miles to the employment exchange at Cross Hands.

I stood in the queue to sign on and collect my dole.

This made me feel wretched. People recognised me and I felt a sense of shame. It had been a part of my upbringing and background that work was all-important, that there was an essential dignity in it, that it was through being a worker that you earned the respect of friends and neighbours. Work had a capital W – and to say about a man 'He's a good worker' was an indication of respect. All this was in my mind as I stood in the dole queue. I was out of work for about six weeks and I hated it; it was an experience that left a mark, and a sympathy for men out of work, that endures.

It was at this time of personal low ebb that the fat carrot of Rugby League was dangled.

It wasn't the first time. The Rugby League clubs keep a close watch on the Union game and players who do very well can expect to receive an offer to turn professional. As a fly-half playing for Llanelli I was naturally noticed and at the time I had been in college there had been a fair amount of gossip in the newspapers about League clubs being interested in me.

'Wigan and St Helen's are keen to sign Barry John,' the columnists had said.

For a while it was just newspaper speculation, for I heard from no one. But, at last, two smartly-dressed men called at my home in Cefneithin and, as soon as they said 'Good morning' in crisp Lancashire, I knew the purpose of their mission. The conversation did not proceed far because I told them firmly that I was in college and wanted to qualify as a teacher.

The next approach was from Wigan. Two directors of the club came to Trinity College at ten o'clock on a Sunday morning and found me, frankly, not at my best. I had been up late and, when the two northern men roused me, I shuffled to the door, sticky-eyed and with a blanket slung around my bent shoulders. These men were used to the tough and giant players of the north; here in front of them they saw a grey-faced ten-and-a-half stone young man who didn't look fit enough to crack the shell of his breakfast egg. I told them that I wanted to finish my studies and play for Wales, but they persisted gently and asked: 'How much do you want?'

I didn't know what to say; it isn't easy for a player to assess his own cash value. I said, laying it on a bit, that I would guarantee them three dropped-goals a match – how much was that worth? They would not commit themselves, and when they saw that I was far from enthusiastic about turning professional, they left.

A few months after this I was in a group of students from the college who were called to a school in Carmarthen to pick up broken glass from the swimming pool.

John and Mike Gibson pursue the loose ball in the third Test at Wellington,
July 31, 1971

John attempts to charge down a clearing kick by New Zealand half-back Sid Going in the fourth Test at Auckland, August 14, 1971

John is tackled by P. Cadle of the Saracens (above) but touches the dropped ball first to score (below)

Some hooligans had thrown smashed bottles in and we volunteered to dive for the pieces. After one dive I surfaced and placed some broken glass on the pool side, just in front of two pairs of shiny shoes. I looked up, and there, looking down, were two men with neat suits. They said they were from Wigan and I clambered out for a chat. I made it clear that I wasn't keen to move . . .

. . . but now, back from South Africa, out of work and a little bitter, I was really vulnerable and interested.

A large and gleaming limousine drew up outside Number 14, Heol Tabernacl, and two men came into our front room for a chat. They were from St Helen's, the major Lancashire club, and, over a cup of tea, they outlined their offer. Eight thousand five hundred pounds tax free, as a signing-on fee; match fees guaranteeing me at least one thousand five hundred pounds a year – plus a teaching job. I was tempted. It sounded like the answer to all my problems. For one thing, I was broke.

I asked my visitors for time to think and, later, talked it all over with Jan. She was teaching at a private school in Swansea at that time and I knew that she would not leave Wales gladly, any more than I would. We visualised ourselves driving up and down the motorways to keep in touch with Wales and our families and friends. But Jan never put any pressure on me. In the end it would be my decision and I knew that I could count on her coming with me if I decided to burn the bridges and get some security in the north of England.

I dithered for a few days, weighing it all up, then took Jan's car and drove to Hereford for a meeting with some of St Helen's directors. We all had lunch in a hotel.

It was enjoyable and, when the meal was over, a

contract was laid in front of me. I read through it quickly.
An expensive fountain pen was proffered – and I took it to
sign my name and change my life. But it hovered over the
paper. My mind was racing. Until that second I had not
appreciated how much Wales meant to me, how strongly
rooted I was in it. I was a Welshman, and I felt I couldn't
give everything up. I drew back at last and returned the
fountain pen.

'I'd like another week to think about it. I'll give you a
ring with a final decision.'

I was sitting at home a day or two later, brooding over
the situation, when our neighbour, Mrs Delyth Nicholas,
came in to say there was a telephone call for me. I went
next door. David Coleman was on the line. He was
collecting material for his *Sportsnight* programme on BBC
television. 'Is what Cliff Morgan says true – that you are
on the dole?' I told him the story. And on his programme
that night he talked about the rugby player who had given
up his job to play for the British Lions and was now out
of work.

Of course, that was a bit of luck for me: few unemployed
men get a Situation Wanted advertisement like that. I felt
that something would come from it and I told my mother
that I would not pick and choose – I would take the first
job offered to me. In the meantime I telephoned St
Helen's Rugby League club and told them I had decided
to stay in Wales.

Then I met Gwynne Walters, the international referee.
He told me the Forward Trust finance house, of which he
was area manager, was on the lookout for representatives.
I expressed interest and a couple of weeks later my
application for a job was accepted. I had no idea of what

a finance representative did, but I was willing to learn very quickly.

I packed my suitcase, put on my best suit and journeyed by bus to Cardiff. At that time I did not know Cardiff at all well and had no idea where the Forward Trust office was. I got off the bus and jumped into a taxi in a nearby rank. Now that I was an employed man again I felt entitled to this small luxury. 'Where to, chief?' the driver said, starting the car and moving off. 'Forward Trust, Greyfriars Road,' I said, in what I hoped was an executive tone. He sighed, pulled into the kerb and said: 'Are you pulling my leg? It's less than fifty yards away.' I took the hint – and walked to work.

After a few days I knew that I had arrived in the large world of business. It was an interesting experience because I felt I was finding my way through a jungle and I began to make new friends – and meet a few sharp characters – on the way. For the first time in my life I felt I was in the adult world. I had been a pupil, then a student, and then for a short while, a schoolmaster, and my life had been governed by terms and school holidays. I had been abroad, but rugby tours are slightly unreal, albeit exciting, experiences. I realised that my view of life had been rather constricted and I enjoyed my new job because it kept me in touch with many new people and their views, and gave me a fresh slant on life. Wynne Jones, the manager of the Forward Trust office in Cardiff, gave me a good grounding in the finance world, and I was helped by the other reps, but I was never an outstanding representative. I was simply not ambitious enough. Wynne was mad about rugby and was very tolerant in allowing me all the time I needed to play and to train. As long as I achieved my business targets every month – and I soon learned how to do that – the arrangement worked very smoothly.

One part of the job I disliked was seeing people who had fallen behind with their hire-purchase instalments. Some of them recognised me and that heightened the embarrassment for both of us.

'Is this how you earn your living then – chasing up debts?' someone said to me. And others said as much with the looks they gave me. 'Hope you bloody lose on Saturday!' was one of the parting shots I got from a customer.

I remember going into a shop in one of the valleys of Glamorgan to see the proprietor about the repayment of his loan. He had fallen a little behind. I faced up to the fact that I would hate every second of it, and went in.

'Now I'm very busy at the moment, Mr John,' he said. 'Can you come back in ten minutes?'

I agreed. When I returned it was clear that he had broadcast the news that I was in town. The shop was bulging with small boys, all buying sweets and comics as they awaited my arrival. The shopkeeper smiled as the cash register rang and the boys hemmed me in, demanding to have their autograph books signed.

'A few more visits like this, Mr John, and we'll have nothing to worry about.'

For almost a year I worked in the Rhondda valleys and the surrounding district, as assistant to Dewi Jones, and I loved every minute of it. The Rhondda has been knocked about a bit but it has an atmosphere of history that I was very aware of as I drove through the streets of terraced houses and little shops. It has retained quite a lot of the old community feeling and I always felt at home. The

Rhondda sense of humour is something special and it lightened the rare dull days.

In 1969 Wales had a great season. We carried off the Triple Crown for the eleventh time and I think that our first victory, over England at Cardiff, can be seen as the genuine beginning of the so-called modern 'golden age' in Welsh rugby. Our attacks worked well and I felt very confident, knowing exactly what I would do when I had the ball.

I dropped a goal early on and then, with a thirty-yard run, went over for a try just as I was being tackled; some critics have called it my best try and it was certainly one of the scores that I care to remember. Because of the way we played in this match we had a feeling of excitement about the future.

Our next international, though, against Scotland at Murrayfield, was not so satisfying. We won – but the Scots were really stubborn and made us struggle hard.

Ireland came to Cardiff Arms Park and were a little easier to beat. This was my fourteenth international and I think I gave one of the best performances of my career. I was on top of the situation and felt that I had become, at last, a complete fly-half, attacking and defending.

I packed my bags for the Wales tour of New Zealand and looked forward eagerly to six enjoyable weeks away.

7. All Black Blues

As it turned out the New Zealand tour was to be a dismal
low tide for Welsh rugby football. The smiles we gave as
we boarded the jet at Heathrow were soon to be wiped
off – torn off – our faces, and our faces rubbed in the mud.

The first mistake – as we can see in hindsight – was that
our party of players and Welsh Rugby Union officials
flew non-stop to New Zealand. The journey took thirty-six
hours and we were very tired, having had no proper
sleep, when we arrived at Auckland about seven o'clock
in the evening.

There was a huge welcoming party there – shouts and
cheers, Red Dragons on sticks, rosettes, and the sound of
'Calon Lan' and 'Mae Hen Wlad Fy Nhadau', our national
anthem. But to most of us it was little more than a blur of
colour and sound. We were zombies, out on our feet. I saw
Keith Jarrett in a chair, chatting with some people, and,
quite suddenly, in the middle of the conversation, he
slumped back fast asleep.

Within ninety minutes of landing in Auckland we were
in the air again, flying one hundred and fifty miles south-
wards to New Plymouth, on the west coast of Taranaki
province. From the airport we were driven to our hotel –
and there was another large and patriotic crowd: it
seemed to be the entire population of the town. We spent

some time on the balcony, waving and chatting, then fell gratefully into our beds. That night a slight earth tremor rumbled and disturbed the town. But not one of us heard it.

The next morning Clive Rowlands, our coach, and Handel Rogers, our manager, could see we were in pretty poor condition and did not insist on a work-out. But two days later, we were due to play Taranaki, and three days after that we were to face the All Blacks in the first Test at Christchurch.

Gareth and I did not play in the Taranaki match, so that we could reserve our strength for the big match. We noticed how tired the forwards looked – their legs were like rubber – and we were lucky to draw the match. Yet within days we were to take on the world champions. Now Taranaki are a very strong side and what we were doing was the equivalent of the All Blacks coming to Britain and within a week of touch-down taking on both a top side like Llanelli and the Welsh team. It was just foolishness.

We flew down to Christchurch in the South Island for the first Test. I still felt tired, like most of the boys, and I had to brace myself. In front of a huge crowd the All Blacks did well: they flattened the Welsh forwards and worked for and deserved their breaks. We missed our chances and lost by nineteen points to nil. With a score line like that what is there left to say? I felt that in the circumstances I had played reasonably well, but when I got the newspapers next morning I saw that the reporters did not share my opinion.

Chastened, we departed for Carisbrook to play our match with Otago province. It was bitterly cold when we arrived and I put on three sweaters. We were expecting a particularly tough match because Otago have a brilliant record against touring teams and they had beaten the three previous British Lions touring sides.

Nevertheless I was looking forward to the clash. Like the rest of the party I wanted to play my part in recovering some of the prestige we had lost in Christchurch. Also, the Otago fly-half Earl Kurton, was a really first-class player and had been written about a good deal. I wanted to examine his technique at close quarters and show that I was the boss. I did. I pulled out the stops and so did the rest of the team. We were very satisfied with a win by twenty-seven points to nine. We returned to the North Island to play Wellington – another good side – on the following Saturday and we won by eleven points to six. Our forwards, though, failed to do themselves justice in the country where good forward play is really important and is admired. After the tour our critics said the Wales forwards were the worst they had seen in a touring party. But that sort of criticism was unfair to many players; and we could not have been a really bad side to have beaten Otago and Wellington in the space of four days.

The second Test in Auckland would be, we all knew, a real test. The odds were stacked against us but one thing we didn't reckon with was the referee: no one, before or since, has so inflamed my temper as that man. And I do not easily lose my temper.

For the first dozen minutes or so Wales played well. We had decided in our pre-match tactics talks to move the ball away from the pack as quickly as we could, making the game more open. This paid dividends almost at once. We took the lead.

And then, as the match was developing, Mr Pat

Murphy, the referee, started to blow his whistle on – or so it looked to many of us – the slightest petty pretext. I must admit that it is difficult for me to write objectively about this because, although the passage of time has enabled me to look at the events a little more dispassionately, my temperature still tends to rise when I think about the second Test.

We all accepted that there would be slightly different interpretations of the rules, that referees are human and fallible after all, but Mr Murphy ruined the match and, frankly, we felt cheated. He blew his whistle for no reason at all, it often seemed to us.

I became so wild at his decisions that I lost my head and said some terrible things to him. He should have sent me off. Any other referee would have. But he pretended not to hear.

At one point, with the game halted yet again, I snarled at him: 'For God's sake, Pat, pull yourself together.'

Now this kind of thing is not good for the other players in the side. It is a kind of mutiny and is unsettling. John Dawes realised this and moved over to me and said: 'Shut up, Barry, for God's sake, before this spreads through the team.'

But by half-time John himself was exasperated enough to demand through tight lips: 'What on earth is going on here?'

And I was beside myself, seething in a cloud of rage, with my sense of control vanished. I yapped and snapped at the referee, cursed and complained to his face. But he seemed not to hear and ignored me.

The New Zealanders whipped us thoroughly by thirty-three points to twelve. It was the first time in forty-five years that a country had scored thirty points against Wales. We imagined the sense of shock there would be among the Welsh fans listening to their radios at three o'clock in the morning, and the quiet inquests in the pits, factories and offices. New Zealand players trotted over to us as we trooped off, heads down. 'Sorry, lads,' they said. They were apologising for the referee.

Well, it's only a game, I suppose – and you should only whisper a sentiment like that in some parts of Wales – but that was the worst exhibition of refereeing I have witnessed. The match reports criticised Mr Murphy too. I find it hard to forgive him.

As for myself I played badly; it was my worst performance in top class rugby. Without Murphy we certainly would not have beaten the All Blacks, for they were without question the far better side. But at least we would have made a decent match of it. We were whistled out of the match.

We flew out of New Zealand with some relief, our tails between our legs, beaten, embarrassed and with the reputation of Welsh rugby tarnished. Of all of us, I suppose, only Barry Llewellyn had come out of the tour with distinction. Don Clark, the ex-New Zealand fullback and now sports writer, said we were the worst touring side he had seen in New Zealand and we could not disagree.

The tour programme had been too packed and too rushed. The Welsh Rugby Union must have been crazy to have accepted a schedule like that. For all of us in Welsh rugby it was a very expensive lesson. Visiting sides are at a great disadvantage in short tours.

So we were glad to leave New Zealand and fly across the

Tasman Sea to Sydney. We stayed there a week – not an agreeable experience, unfortunately, for the weather was bad and the hotel was about to be demolished.

Rugby Union in Australia does not have the sort of aura and following that it has in New Zealand or Wales or France and we did not feel the usual kind of tension before our one match with the Australians. But they provided stiff opposition on a muddy pitch and we had to fight hard to win by nineteen points to sixteen.

Relief from the rain and the grey clouds, both real and figurative, was at hand. We climbed into a jet at Sydney airport and flew two thousand five hundred miles across the south Pacific to Fiji and to the sunshine and to the happy smiling faces of the islanders. The school children had been given a holiday to greet us and we went to an offshore island to receive a ceremonial welcome from a paramount chief.

We spent a glorious week in Fiji and put our sagging self-respect out in the sun to heal a little.

Fiji is the most colourful, exotic, *different*, rugby-playing country. Fijians love their rugby and they play it with enormous energy and humour and follow it avidly. They seemed to know us all and we were fêted as stars. As we travelled about in a windowless bus they waved and shouted and grinned.

We stayed at a hotel in Suva, the capital, and relaxed beside a swimming pool during the hot afternoons. At night we watched the dancers and revelled in the beat of drums.

One morning we went out training and there was a sudden storm of rain. It was like an exhilarating lukewarm shower and we ran around half-naked, laughing and shouting at the tops of our voices. Then the frogs came out to play; frogs as large as dinner plates, croaking and leaping among us. The sight of them was enough to scare Gerald Davies: he completed his training with a high-speed sprint back to the dressing rooms.

We played only one match in Fiji and I was reserve and sat it out. The stadium was a startling contrast to those grounds in the valleys of Wales. This one was surrounded by waving palms and from the stand you could see the surf breaking on the dazzling beach. The stadium was packed with twenty-four thousand chattering and laughing people. Many of them had journeyed for days, in sailing boats and motor boats, from the outlying islands, just to see the match. It was scorching hot and a brass band in scarlet uniforms paraded on the pitch. It was a fiesta day.

The Fijians gave us a quick surprise: Fred Allen, the former All Blacks player, had travelled to the islands to coach the local team and they had listened very intently to his advice. They attacked smartly on the blind side and scored. But by half-time Wales were three points in front and in the second half wore the Fijians down.

Three minutes after the final whistle, the Fiji players, proudly wearing their swopped Welsh shirts, and with their boots strung around their necks, were at the bar enjoying a drink. We joined them and, after a while, returned to our hotel to change for a reception. The Fijians simply strolled out across the fields in the late sunshine to go home and get changed.

The islanders had made us feel so much at home, and so welcome, that it was a wrench for us to leave at last. We flew over the Pacific to Honolulu and then to San Francisco, staying overnight before going on to New York and London.

Back in Wales we felt depressed. We were neither conquerors nor heroes. I was glad, therefore, to go to Spain for two weeks with Jan and her family. My father-in-law wanted to keep in touch with the news of Wales and had the *Western Mail* posted out to him. Reading it one day I saw that my grandmother had died in Cefneithin. She had been known for many years as Mam Low and her home had been something of a first-aid post for the village. She seemed to know exactly how to soothe burns, cuts and bruises and if you had a splinter you went to Mam Low. She patched up the small wounds and sometimes handed out her distilled wisdom. She had been a part of my boyhood and here, on this sunny beach, I felt a sense of loss.

In September Jan and I were married at St Mary's Church in Swansea. My best man was Peter Davies, who had been with me at college and who had pleaded with a lecturer for permission for a group of us to go out after hours to celebrate my selection for the Welsh team. A year or so before our wedding day I had told Jan, rather loftily, that rugby would have to come before romance and she would have to take a back seat while I concentrated on my playing career. She didn't bat an eyelid – well, not in front of me. I did concentrate on rugby for a while, but one day, as I was going to Cardiff station to catch a train, I met Jan. She was going down to Swansea and we had a long talk on the journey. I decided that any sensible man could easily make room for both rugby and romance. We became engaged shortly afterwards. Marriage gave my life the kind of direction it needed; I had rugby and a job, but no real root. I was glad to settle down.

8. Grand Slam

The best try I ever scored was in the best match I ever played in: France v. Wales at the old Colombes stadium in Paris in March 1971, the culminating match of a great season for Welsh rugby.

I always enjoy watching the French in action on the rugby field, and I always loved playing against them, particularly in France. I admire their grace and enthusiasm and sheer delight in playing beautiful rugby, especially when they are winning.

If, during my ten years in top-class rugby, I could have changed my nationality for just one match, I would have chosen to play for France . . . alongside men like Villepreux, Barrau, Maso, Lux, Bertranne, Cantoni and others . . . with the aroma of garlic and Gauloises in the stadium air and the 'Marseillaise' in my ears.

For the French bring to rugby a special quality of enjoyment. They get really passionate about it. When Welshmen score a try they walk away quietly, perhaps acknowledging the modest pats on the back from their team-mates. But Frenchmen exult. When they score they don't have much use for modesty. They shout and leap as if asking, with un-selfconscious pride and pleasure: 'Aren't we great?'

Wales had not won in France since 1956–7 and, of

course, we were after the Grand Slam. It was also our last match at the Colombes stadium – before internationals in Paris moved to the Parc des Princes – and so we had three reasons for wanting to do well as we ran up the long tunnel into the circle of daylight and the crackling atmosphere created by a crowd of Frenchmen on their toes to see a great battle.

The important factor in matches against France is to do well in the first twenty minutes. If the French get the upper hand in this crucial period the match is lost.

The secret is to break up the Frenchmen's patterns of play, to disorganise and annoy them, to keep their possession down to a minimum, to tackle, tackle constantly.

With the ball in their hands the French are dancers, creating lovely and fluid movements, delighting the eye. Their weakness is that they are not always good at the donkey work of rugby. So when the ball came out of the scrum to me I would place it between the full-back and the centres, making them turn round, and causing disarray. Reporters and spectators have complained about a lack of pattern and direction in internationals with France. We in the Welsh team worked hard to create this untidiness as our prime battle tactic. On the rugby field, as in the kitchen, the French can be masters, with touches of genius, but who does the lowly work, like peeling the potatoes? I made it one of my tasks to give them rugby potatoes to peel.

In this match the French started with the wind in their favour and got a lot of ball in the first few minutes. We were like torpedoes, tackling hard to break up the patterns and get them on the fidget. I did not make my reputation in rugby as a tackler, but I believe I tackled more in this match than in all my other internationals put together.

It was during one of these tackles that my nose was broken. Benoit Dauga, the big second row forward, fought his way almost to the try line but was stopped close to the corner flag. He was upright, but swaying, as I jumped at him. Had he fallen to his left he would have scored a try; to his right he would be in touch. I leaped to push him into touch and as we both fell I got underneath him and his elbow accidentally crashed on to my nose.

I went off the field for attention. On the touchline a French doctor looked at my nose, which was bent down over my face, and suddenly pulled it hard. There was a click and a burst of pain. But it was straight. Cotton wool was pushed into my nostrils to staunch the flow of blood and I went back to the game.

I was feeling hazy and for a few minutes played by instinct. Our incessant tackling and undermining of the French defence began to pay off. They felt penned and began to be rattled. Gareth scored a try and I kicked a penalty to give Wales a six points to five lead.

And then came my great chance. There was a set-piece scrum, with the backs marking each other carefully, and Jeff Young got the ball against the head. Gareth shot it out to me. I saw that Berot, the fly-half, was slightly out of position and as I accelerated I saw the others bearing down on me. I ran straight at Bertranne, the inside-centre, but he started to move across and I deduced that he was anticipating I would pass to John Dawes. Berot was within feet of me now, moving very fast, but I sensed that we already had the try – it would be me or John. In an instant I changed the course of my sweeping run and beat Berot:

George Best and Barry John

Barry John is presented to Princess Anne at the opening of the new Sports Centre at Cardiff

John races away with the ball to go on and score for the International XV
against the Saracens

J. McLaughlan of Scotland tackled by John in the match against Scotland
in February, 1972

I felt his outstretched fingers running down my back as I went over for the try. For me it crowned a good personal performance, a complete performance in terms of attacking and covering.

Well, the French are most difficult to beat in Paris and this was clearly a glorious way to achieve the Grand Slam for the sixth time. The champagne and the celebration dinner helped to relieve the discomfort I felt from my aching and throbbing nose. We had that sense of fulfilment that comes from completing a mission successfully.

What made the celebration even more enjoyable was the sportsmanship of the French players and their officials. They love winning, of course, but if they have played well and are beaten in a great game they are just as happy.

As the 1970–1 season had progressed towards this climax, it had become clear that Wales was an outstanding side. We won our first championship match, against a nondescript England side at Cardiff Arms Park, easily enough, and I scored two dropped goals, starting me off on the accumulation of sixty-six points in my last seven matches for Wales. All the internationals are important, of course, but the Welsh team gets a special satisfaction out of beating England, the old enemy. In a romantic sense, I suppose, we are warriors going out to get some revenge for the hurts caused to us centuries ago, Welshmen kicking their Saxon conquerors.

The match against Scotland was one of the most amazing I have played in. It was a classic match and the real character of the Welsh side showed through. Both teams were very anxious to avoid wasting even a second of the precious battle time. When points were scored there was no hanging about – everyone dived straight back into the action. At one stage we gave away a silly try, but there was no recrimination or muttering: we really believed in ourselves as a team. Though it must be said that we did cut things a little fine – nineteen points to eighteen after eighty minutes of cut-throat rugby!

I suffered an injury to my neck and head when I went over for a try. I was tackled hard by Billy Steel and felt a jarring thud as I hit the ground clumsily. For some periods of the match I was moving around the field instinctively; I felt hazy and after the match there were several periods of play that I could not recall. When I drove to work in Cardiff the following Monday morning I found I could not steer properly and later in the day, while making a phone call to the office, I found myself sliding to the floor. I went to my doctor and he took me to hospital for X-rays. Fortunately there was no fracture, but I had severe bruising and I felt unwell for some time.

The Irish team came to Cardiff for our third championship match and got off to a cracking start, winning plenty of possession. We didn't get enough of the ball to control the match but, on the first occasion we did get good ball, Gerald Davies scored one of his specials. I don't know how he does it sometimes. I dropped a goal, rather luckily because I did not hit the ball squarely, and then a penalty. At half-time we were three points in the lead although the Irish had rather pushed us about the Arms Park. That lead gave us the psychological fillip we needed and we had things more our own way.

We deserved the Triple Crown. We were a well-balanced side able to fight hard when the pressure was strong, and we were flexible and original. We had some luck, of course. Rugby has an egg-shaped ball and its bounce is not predictable. Like the throw of a dice, it can run against you, but for our team that season it generally bounced kindly. Still, you have to be good enough to capitalise on the bounce when it is to your advantage, and we did not miss many opportunities.

Now we had the match against France to look forward to and the newspapers were full of Grand Slam talk. We did not remain aloof from all the speculation and the general buzz of excitement: the idea of pulling off the Grand Slam got into our blood. Wales had last done it in 1952.

Ten days before the match with France the British Lions touring party was announced. I think this was unfortunate for two reasons. A number of players in the Welsh team were selected and they had to travel to France and play with team-mates, some of whom had had hopes that were not now realised. It says much for the element of common sense in this Welsh side that those who had been selected for the tour made no fuss at all about it when the team met up to go to France. No back-slapping or pumping of hands. We had no wish to accentuate any feelings of disappointment. Another factor was that a player picked for the tour might have held back a fraction to avoid injury that could cost him his place. If one man, with the tour in mind, had held back on one tackle we might have lost the game. It didn't happen – but the Lions selectors might have done better to announce the names after the France and Wales game.

Much of the credit for our success in 1971 belongs with John Dawes, the skipper, the greatest skipper I have played under – and I am certain that other captains would agree. He taught me a great deal about instant decision-making. He never panicked. He took stock quietly and when he made a decision he stuck to it. He knew the exact resources of the team and he was in essence, a general. At the same time he was perhaps the best giver and taker of a pass I have ever played with. His qualities made him the ideal captain for the Lions. He was a model skipper both on and off the field. He gave to the Welsh side, and then to the Lions, a certain stature. He didn't say much on the field and he expressed appreciation with a quiet 'Well done, feller!' He didn't say it often, reserving it for something outstanding, and so it was valued.

Our performance in 1971 was a considerable contrast to our performance in the season before. The South African tourists were here and Wales played them at Cardiff in the most miserable conditions. The Arms Park was a quagmire, it was bitterly cold and there was driving rain. It was more like trench warfare than rugby and we were happy enough to draw.

Earlier in the season, I had hoped to be able to play for Cardiff against the Springboks, but I fractured a rib while playing for the Barbarians at Oxford and had to rest for six weeks. In fact I never played for Cardiff against a touring side, something I regret.

Wales did not play at all well against Scotland at Cardiff in February. We should have been beaten, really. And we maybe should have been beaten by England at Twickenham later that month. We were trailing thirteen points to three when Gareth injured a hamstring muscle and went off. All seemed lost, but Chico Hopkins came on, with twenty-eight minutes to go, to claim his first cap and make the match his own. Maybe he had seen from the touchline what was wrong with us. Anyway he worked beautifully and inspired backs and forwards alike. I scored a try, then Chico made one for John Williams, then he scooped up the ball when it ran loose from a line out and he dived through to bring us one point behind England. None of us could bear to watch when John Williams converted the try. I rounded it all off with a dropped goal.

Thus we went off to Dublin with supporters in Wales excitedly talking in terms of the Triple Crown. But we were aware that we had been winning because our opponents had been making mistakes. The Triple Crown was never on. Ireland did not let us off the hook and beat us fourteen points to nil. The Welsh Rugby Union made a mistake in booking us into a hotel some way out of Dublin, for that deprived us of the atmosphere created by supporters. We only came into contact with the big match atmosphere when we ran out on to the pitch. But no excuses. Ireland smashed us, and rightly exposed all the faults in the Welsh team. The important thing was that we learned the lessons.

9. Pride of Lions

For some time I was in two minds about accepting the invitation to go on the British Lions tour to New Zealand. On one hand I was fairly happy with my rugby achievements – I had been to South Africa as a Lion, I had toured New Zealand with the Welsh side and I had been in the Wales Grand Slam team. What is more, I am a home bird. I like my own fireside and I did not want to leave Jan and Kate, then nine months old, for three and a half months. On the other hand, though, I felt in my bones that the Lions tour would be a momentous one, with great battles. The party would be an outstanding group of players; it would obviously have a strong Welsh accent and Carwyn James would be coach. All of these factors began to tip the scale as I paced about the house. Jan told me not to dither. 'For heaven's sake, Barry, you'll have to go. You'll be impossible to live with if you don't.'

She was right, of course.

I was in good form and I had the feeling it would last. I accepted enthusiastically.

It was exciting to be going on a Lions tour that had the feeling of a well-planned expedition about it. We weren't a crowd of amateurs flying off for a spot of fun and travel; we were a task force with a mission.

At the heart of the whole enterprise was good management, in the form of Doug Smith and Carwyn. Players rely a lot on the manager. He lifts loads from them and has to be able to stand up to the varied pressures of a tour without flinching. He has to be a good organiser, sociable, thick-skinned, broadminded, a diplomat to the marrow, blessed with the ability to make a fine speech at two seconds' notice, able to withstand endless hospitality without apparent ill-effect, a born problem-shrinker.

In short, he has to be a Doug Smith.

Doug is a doctor, a Scot with a lovely accent, and has a way of telling a story so that we used to look forward to hearing him speak at a function. He played soccer for Aberdeen at one time and had a tremendous kick – as we discovered when he belted a ball at us in our knockabouts. Doug grew in stature as the tour went on, figuratively and physically. We players watched as, week by week, he let out his belt notch by notch. Chico Hopkins used to say that the management had worked out a punishment for any player missing an important kick: he would have to run twenty yards with Doug on his back!

There was no formal discipline imposed by the management; no rules were laid down and we were treated as individuals. In South Africa in 1968 there had been some hooliganism, some shirt-burning and crockery smashing, but there was none in New Zealand. The only time I saw something smashed was at the Southern Cross Hotel in Dunedin, during the evening after the first Test. The hotel had some beautiful chandeliers in one of its public rooms and, quite unexpectedly, one of the New Zealanders kicked a ball into the air and broke one. The Lions got the blame.

In fact, although there was boisterous behaviour in

private, we never felt the need to run wild. Perhaps it was because we were a well-integrated and successful party – and success breeds happiness. In my early letters home to Jan I wrote that the people in the tour group seemed to be on the same wave-length, that there was a fundamental contentment and confidence. This was one of the spin-offs from coaching. We knew each other well and we had met each other's wives and girl friends. There was not, for instance, any of the nervous indecision I felt when I first played for Wales – when I agonised over the question of whether I should call Alan Pask, the skipper, Mr Pask or Alan. And when I went to South Africa I tortured myself with the problem of how to address the great Syd Millar: Mr Millar might have sounded artificially respectful, Sydney might have been too pushing, and Syd might have been out-and-out brashness.

Another good aspect of the New Zealand tour was the party's good relationship with newspapermen and broadcasters. In South Africa we had been warned to be very careful about what we said to the Press, but on this tour of 1971 there were no restrictions and we felt able to talk frankly with reporters. I never refused an interview. Our off-the-record confidences were respected so that an atmosphere of trust developed. Our relationship with the Press was, in my view, an important part of the success of the tour. It helped us to get the New Zealand public on our side.

It is only occasionally that rugby players get thrown together for a period of nearly four months. We were from many different backgrounds and of different outlooks – professional, artisan, middle class, working class, Scots, Irish, Welsh, English, all with our idiosyncrasies. The fact that we lived closely together without tension for all that time – I remember only one argument between two players and that was not serious – speaks volumes. It says much for the tolerance and sense of humour and common sense of each player and official. And that, of course, is a reflection on the care taken by the selectors. It is not readily appreciated by the public that, however good at rugby a player might be, he might not necessarily make a good tourist. And I should also say that those players on the tour who did not make the Test teams and who played only a few times made as large a contribution to the success of the whole enterprise as those who played often, because they were good tourists and put all they had into the common cause. Bob Hiller, for example, did not play in the Tests, but he scored a lot of points in other matches, particularly mid-week ones, and this contributes much to morale. It might be imagined that some players felt disappointed about being left out of teams, but in fact there was no resentment. The players trusted the management. For all of us one of the important aspects of the tour was that we had Carwyn James as coach. For me his presence was particularly important because he has had a considerable influence on my life, as player, coach and man.

As I've already written, he was a boyhood hero of mine and I tried to adopt his calm attitude to rugby. On this tour I got to know him really well – and we developed a friendly rivalry in games of snooker. We played as often as we could in New Zealand and we carry on the 'battle' as often as we can today.

Carwyn never undermined his position as coach by trying to be 'one of the boys'. He retained his authority always but never became aloof or authoritarian. He knew how to handle us – when to push this player, when to hold back with that player. When he got up to speak to us we always concentrated, quiet as mice, because we knew he was telling us how to win the matches. His approach was quiet and reasoned. He regarded us as inflammable fuel and was anxious not to throw in the spark prematurely.

Carwyn is not only a rugby man, he is a political one as well. He is a member of Plaid Cymru, the Welsh nationalist party, and has stood as a Parliamentary candidate. His politics are not empty words, or slogans; what he says, he feels sincerely. In a nutshell, he cares deeply for Wales and it is everything to him. He knows the country and its language and literature thoroughly. He believes that as a basis for national and international understanding, men should get to know and understand their own background and locality and community, and from this base build up their knowledge and develop an understanding of the wider world; and this seems to me to be good sense.

He would never introduce politics into conversations. He would only discuss the subject if it was introduced by someone else, and only if the atmosphere was serious. Carwyn is an impressive talker and if you meet him for only a minute or two you will remember something he said.

There was a memorable evening in Masterton – Gerald Davies, Gareth, Carwyn and I dined together and this was unusual because the Welsh, the Scots, the Irish and the English rarely got into 'ethnic' groups on the tour. We had a wonderful discussion, for Carwyn is a master of debate – and we also had claret. Our first bottle was ice-cold and we remarked on this to the waiter. When we ordered another bottle the wine fountained out as the cork was withdrawn. The bottle had been put into a pan of water and heated on a stove.

The preliminary to a Lions tour is the meeting and warm-up at Eastbourne. This was a ritual I loathed, like most of the other boys. Eastbourne is not much more than a public showing, a parade, with the players running around in smart track suits. But all the time you are scared stiff that you will put your foot into a pot-hole and cause an injury that will put you out of the tour – you are not a Lion until the plane takes off. Far better, in my view, to meet in London for a dinner and then fly out, using the time that is now spent in Eastbourne on acclimatisation in the host country.

Every tourist has to make some mental preparation before embarking on the adventure. Personally, I wound up a kind of mental clock that would stop on the last day of the tour; for three and a half months I would devote myself wholeheartedly to the tour, but the minute it finished I wanted to forget rugby. If somebody had asked me to play a game two or three days after the tour I would have had neither the physical nor mental equipment.

Personal considerations have to be put aside as far as possible and players have to think in terms of group living. Some players adapt very easily to touring; others dislike living out of suitcases. It is amazing, really, how much a trivial matter like a missing shirt can upset a player on tour. The small things of day to day existence sometimes assume a great importance. If anyone had wanted to upset me on tour he need only have sabotaged the laundry. Because there is nervous tension the organisation must not falter and the behind-the-scenes work of the management and the baggage master is absolutely critical to success.

Talking about laundry reminds me that several times during the New Zealand tour I received my clean shirts from the laundry girls – plus autograph books and addressed envelopes with notes begging: 'Please sign the books and send us photographs.' On one occasion a shirt was even missing from my small batch, but there was a blackmail note saying: 'Your shirt is safe. Please sign your autograph and send it to us.' And, sure enough, I got my shirt back.

After leaving London on the seventh of May, we stopped off at Hong Kong – I enjoyed my visit and I wish it had been three times as long – and then flew down to Brisbane for the first of our two matches in Australia. I was glad that I did not play in the first one, against Queensland, because, like most of the boys, I was still tired after the long flight. The Australia matches are fitted – some would say squeezed – into the tour with the aim of showing the Rugby Union flag and helping to raise money for the game. The problem for the tourists is that rugby is a very hard game in Australia, and the grounds are usually hard, too. Queensland beat us in our first match but we defeated New South Wales – virtually the Australian Test side – before flying to New Zealand. Thank God that we had a week to rest when we arrived there.

I scored three penalties, a dropped goal and two conversions in our win over Counties and Thames Valley, our first match in New Zealand. Our forwards showed up well, but I felt a little dissatisfied with my own performance, and with the backs as a unit. My balance wasn't what it should have been – probably my studs were not long enough. Though my team-mates ribbed me and said the new gum shield I was wearing was too heavy and was making me fall over.

There were ten provincial matches before the first Test, and I played in five of them, scoring seventy-three points. Because of a back injury I didn't play in the match against Canterbury, which was just as well because I might have had my face punched in like some of the other boys. As it was I felt bruised and sore just watching. I was sitting in the stand, about forty yards from the touchline, but I could see clearly that the Canterbury side had gone on to the field with the idea of punching the Lions out of the match.

Now in a game like rugby one accepts that there will be provocation, that tempers may flare, that someone may snarl: 'I'll break your leg for you . . .' From time to time a punch is thrown. But in the main players are not anxious to be involved in fighting. Rugby remains a clean game. But what we saw at Christchurch, with the Canterbury players cynically using violence as part of their match-plan, horrified me. As I sat in my seat I felt my fists clenching and a wave of anger went through the Lions boys watching. And when I went to the dressing room the scene was terrible. Ray McLoughlin and Sandy Carmichael were so badly hurt that they could take no further part in the tour. Had Sandy been a boxer in the ring, no boxing referee would have let him carry on with the injuries he received at the hands of the Canterbury thugs. Anyway, Canterbury failed to smash us out of the game with fouls and violence. We beat them because we played better rugby, and clean rugby at that. And that gave us some grim satisfaction. All this was only a week before the first Test in Dunedin. There was another match three days later, which the Lions won, so we came to the first Test with an unbeaten record.

My back was still troubling me only a few days before the Test and, with three other players who were on the injury list, I went to Dunedin for hospital treatment. Gareth had hurt a hamstring muscle and he and I were lucky because our injuries responded pretty quickly to treatment.

I was able to get plenty of rest – an ideal build-up to the big match. In the days before an important match I like to be fairly quiet and on my own, slowing down pleasantly. I slept a great deal and went to bed in the afternoons. In fact, throughout the tour, I had a post-lunch sleep two or three times a week and made dreadful threats to the hotel receptionists and telephonists about what I might do if they allowed the phone to ring and disturb me.

On the Wednesday before the big match there was a training session and I could hardly wait to get on to the field. I worked really hard: I wanted to prove to myself that a week's lay-off didn't do me much harm.

A Test match on a tour is a completely different experience to any other kind of match. You anticipate it and get worked up in a way you cannot before a provincial game. You concentrate much harder.

I was certain that we would all play well. By this stage of the tour the forwards knew that they had a great backs division behind them – and we knew we had an outstanding bunch of forwards. A mutual confidence had grown up. What worried me was that, although I knew we would do our best, and our best should be good enough, there might be an invisible and intangible force protecting the All Blacks. On previous occasions I had played against them – for the Barbarians and for East Wales - and the All Blacks had been outplayed. Yet an indefinable 'something' had been on their side and had carried them through.

In the newspapers and on radio and television there was a tremendous build-up to the Test, but we were hardened to ballyhoo and unaffected by it. After all, eleven of the team had played against New Zealand before and, more important, in New Zealand. We were a seasoned crowd of players.

Even so we could hardly fail to be impressed by the enthusiasm and the mounting tide of publicity and speculation. I remember switching on the radio one morning in my room at the Southern Cross Hotel in Dunedin, and finding that the voice of Cliff Morgan filled the air. He was talking to a very noisy and excited crowd of people; it sounded as if a big party was well under way. After a few minutes I realised that the broadcast was coming from the lounge and the bar downstairs!

Just before we left the hotel I rang Jan to say a few re-assuring words. Reassuring – because she associated Test matches with injuries, particularly the broken collar bone I had suffered during the South African tour. I told her we were all in good form and she wasn't to worry. I put the phone down, but five minutes later it rang. Jan was on the line.

'I forgot to wish you good luck. Good luck!'

In the bus from the hotel to the ground the atmosphere

was charged with tension. The team chat in the hotel room had been very edgy – many players couldn't sit still for more than a minute or two without getting up or squirming.

The forwards seemed to tremble with energy. If someone had hung up a punch bag in the centre of the room we would all have walked up to it and, without thinking, hit it as hard as we could.

We knew we had prepared thoroughly, that Carwyn had done his work to the last detail. We knew exactly how we would play and the forwards, in particular, were trained and keyed up for an exceptional experience.

As the bus neared the ground there wasn't much conversation. We all looked at each other. There were no words, but our faces said everything. The looks said: 'I believe you are going to play brilliantly today. I believe in your ability. I believe that this will be your finest game.'

It is an amazing feeling to find that just by looking at another man's face you can transmit, and receive, a certain energy. We felt very much like a family. There were no Welshmen, Englishmen, Scotsmen or Irishmen. Just Lions.

We thought of the hundreds of telegrams and telephone calls we had received, of all the people sitting up and listening to their radios. I had received a telephone call from three fans in London who, obviously slightly tipsy, demanded my assurance that I would score at least twenty points. There had been messages from Members of Parliament and sports personalities.

And there was a cable saying: 'Best of luck, lads. All thinking of you. Joe.' Who Joe was we had no idea, but

John's jinking side-step. M. I. Player attempts a tackle

John punts ahead in the Test against France at Cardiff, March 25, 1972

A place kick, Wales against Scotland at Cardiff, February 5, 1972

The finish of a drop kick in the fourth Test at Auckland, August 14, 1971

the telegram meant a lot to us. It evoked for all of us the image of the anonymous supporter, who had got up early, or stayed up late, to hear the radio commentary.

We were now convinced that the whole of Britain was awake in the small hours, urging us on; and we were determined not to be another Lions team that did well in provincial matches but failed in the Tests. We felt we owed it to the people at home not to fail. More important, we felt we owed it to ourselves.

The coach pulled up at the ground. Chico Hopkins, as he did before every match, started his chant of 'Give us an L, give us an I . . . O, N, S!' And we shouted out 'THE LIONS!' This was our war-cry, leaving the bus and leaving the dressing room.

The New Zealanders attacked us very hard from the kick-off – and after five minutes Gareth had the ill-luck to suffer a recurrence of his hamstring injury. He went off and Chico replaced him – playing in the exuberant fashion that recalled his great first match against England.

I missed a couple of shots at goal in the first half as well as a conversion, and I felt a little annoyed about this. Then in the second half I had a thirty-five yard penalty shot; I made myself relax, but as I ran up I muttered to myself that if I did not score this time I would not kick again on the tour. I was relieved when the ball went between the posts and I scored another penalty a little later. We beat the All Blacks by nine points to three. After we had weathered the fierce onslaught of the first fifteen minutes a feeling of great confidence ran through the Lions because we knew we had held them while they were playing their most powerful rugby. Although they had a great deal of the play they showed us all their cards. We recognised that they had no alternatives and, equally important, they recognised it, too.

One of the more important tasks that I had in this first Test was to make life very difficult for Fergie McCormick, the All Blacks full-back. During the Canterbury match, Carwyn James and I had watched his performance – and when Carwyn said to me: 'Fergie is interesting today, isn't he?' I knew exactly what he meant. Fergie was not getting under the ball properly and he was struggling. I knew that in the Test match I would have to keep his mind solely on defence, give him a hard time and make sure that he would not have any ideas about coming into the line and attacking. I succeeded. I taunted him with my kicks and kept him under a relentless pressure. He missed two penalties and after the match the New Zealand selectors dropped him; that pleased us enormously because Fergie McCormick was a good player and potentially very dangerous.

After our Test victory the celebrations lasted until the small hours, and, for some, beyond. We felt elated, of course, and Doug Smith, our manager, who had been a Lion in the fifties, wore a large grin. We flew off to Queenstown for a short holiday and a series of discussions on our performance in the Test match. Queenstown is a lovely place, a resort ideal for relaxing in. All I wanted to do was sleep. I slept all night, got up for breakfast, played a few games of snooker, slept, got up for the evening meal – and then went back to bed again. It may not be everyone's idea of celebrating, but it suited me.

At the start of the match with New Zealand Universities the following week I needed only six points to equal the record of one hundred points by a tourist in New Zealand set up by Gerry Brand of South Africa in 1937. I did it with two penalties, then went on to get a try, another penalty, a dropped goal and three conversions. At the end of the match I had scored one hundred and fifteen points in eight matches.

When I scored the try that gave me the record, Cliff Morgan, who was doing a commentary on the match, fell off his chair in the excitement. He was the only casualty in the Lions party that travelled back to the hotel in a coach.

Like the other newspaper and radio and television men who accompanied us, Cliff made a great contribution to the success of the tour. For one thing, he is a great tourist himself – and he is one of the most generous men I know. Once, when I was feeling a little dispirited during the season before the Lions tour, he had sent a letter to: 'The greatest fly-half in the world, c/o Cardiff Rugby Club.' Coming from a man who was himself one of the greatest fly-halves of all time, it was a gesture that made my spirits soar.

In the second Test at Christchurch New Zealand beat us by twenty-two points to twelve, capitalising on our errors. Among the Lions there was not the same sense of urgency as had existed before the first Test when we had that determination, that intense ambition, to beat the All Blacks. To our cost we found that the New Zealanders were fighting for their rugby lives in this second Test and were playing close to their best.

They deserved to win but, although we were beaten, we realised that we had more than an even chance of winning the series. For we had created more try-scoring situations than in the first Test match and had won more quality possession – that is, our scrum-half had got possession of the ball with room to manoeuvre, with the extra fraction of a second in which to think, and that meant we were able to play on our toes rather than on our heels. We now saw clearly that what we had to do in the third Test was to eliminate the mistakes in defence – and play as we had never played before.

The third Test, the great test, was at Wellington on the last day of July. The feeling I had before this match was that everything I had done before in rugby would have counted for nothing if we did not win this match. It was going to be the most important match I was ever to play in. I felt we were better than the All Blacks and that we should win; and in the process we could revolutionise rugby thinking.

There was no mid-week fixture and we spent the week at a quiet place called Waitangi. We were much in need of a break for we were threequarters of the way through the tour and players were in danger of becoming fatigued. We needed to get away from rugby and talk about rugby. So we spent the weekend, plus Monday and Tuesday, relaxing and chatting (not about rugby), playing snooker and golf, table tennis and cards, going fishing and getting plenty of glorious sleep, topped up with occasional naps.

The hotel provided pleasant cabarets and Maori evenings to entertain us. But while the players were taking it easy Carwyn was thinking hard, planning the way we should beat the All Blacks. He knew that the prime threat would come from their scrum-half, Sid Going, and his pattern of play with their back row. Sid had been given too much room in the second Test – and Operation Stop

Sid would be crucial in this match. Carwyn took our back row of Derek Quinnell, Mervyn Davies and John Taylor and drilled them hard in the art of containing Going. Derek was the key man in this. He was ordered to 'live with' Sid for the eighty minutes of the match – and he did, with the result that Sid was largely ineffective. And in the Lions camp afterwards Derek's name was mentioned in glowing terms. During the training sessions beforehand Chico Hopkins played the rôle of Sid Going and he bravely bore a lot of hammering from Derek because Carwyn insisted that there should be no play-acting and if Chico got past him Derek would be in trouble.

The main preparation of the backs was in counter-attacking. We split into two sides of three or four each and one would attack along the whole length of the field. John Dawes insisted that we scored a try every time and this meant that the last man with the ball was having to race fifty or sixty yards. We had to be fast and we had to think – the kind of rugby training I liked.

While we were working-up in Waitangi a group of us went for a run along the road with John Dawes. But after a quarter of a mile I was left behind and, lazily, did not feel inclined to finish the run. A lorry came around the bend and I thumbed a lift to the dressing rooms. On the way I stopped for some oranges. And when John and the boys came in, panting and perspiring, I was there, cool, and with a plateful of oranges for them. Some local people who witnessed this bit of fun could hardly believe their eyes: rugby is taken so seriously in New Zealand that many clubs would have had a player on the carpet for doing what I did.

I felt that it was a good thing for the New Zealand

rugby public to see us clowning and enjoying ourselves. I hoped that we persuaded many people that successful rugby and fun could be compatible.

We always looked closely at the newspaper photographs of the All Blacks in training or 'off duty' to see if we could spot a smile. We never did. Every All Black had a long face or a grim expression. Now that's not the way to approach rugby, is it?

Carwyn schooled us individually and collectively, in great detail, on how we should play in the third Test. He was perfectly calm – but he must have been bursting to grab each one of us by the lapels and urge us to do well.

He took great pains. Just before the match he got a detailed weather forecast from the meteorological office in Wellington and, with this in mind, he and John Dawes decided that if John were lucky with the toss we would play with the wind in the first half because the breeze might lessen in the second.

Now John was very lucky with the toss throughout the tour – and when he won it a pre-arranged plan clicked into operation. The two skippers tossed the coin in the dressing rooms, but John always said he would leave the decision about the kick-off and what end to play in until we were out on the field. Then the Lions raced out to the far end of the half they wanted and stayed there, trying to look as if they owned it. John would tell the referee that the Lions opted to kick off and the referee would turn to the opposing skipper to offer him the choice of ends. Every time the skipper looked at the Lions, far away, and decided it would be too much trouble to call us back to change ends. Thus we got the twin advantages of the kick-off and the end we favoured.

Now, in this third Test, John won the toss again – and out we scampered with the orders for a hard and sustained early attack on the All Blacks ringing in our ears.

By this stage of the tour I was well aware that my performance on the field would have a marked effect on the result of the game, simply because I was the team's goal kicker. A few goals could win a game – but a few missed would certainly lose it. The day before the match I had an edgy feeling and, as I ran out on to the pitch at Wellington, I felt a great sense of responsibility. My standard of play throughout the tour had been good, but any player gets the feeling that after a run of good matches he is bound to have a bad one. Is this, I wondered, feeling rather nervous about it as I looked round at the great crowd, going to be the off-day?

I recalled that in the match against New Zealand Universities there had been the inexplicable business of two dropped passes. The passes were from Chico Hopkins and they were excellent, but I put them down all the same. The boys had gaped – I never dropped passes – and the crowd buzzed. I had decided that the best thing to do was to show off a little: I picked up the ball, examined it quizzically and then gave a broad grin to show I was not worried. But, of course, I made damn certain that I didn't drop another one!

My thoughts and slight nervousness were stilled by the whistle – and the match started.

I need not have worried. I was soon closely involved in

our tremendous opening burst. After three minutes Derek Quinnell shot the ball out of a ruck to Mike Gibson. I called for it and gave us the lead with a dropped goal from thirty yards. A few minutes later Gerald Davies scored a tremendous try by the corner flag and I converted, with the ball glancing off the far post. Then Gareth set up an easy try for me, near the posts, and, with the conversion, we had thirteen points in eighteen minutes. We didn't score again, but the New Zealanders were, effectively, already beaten. Our back row played very well, Operation Stop Sid was a success and all of Carwyn's well-laid plans had worked happily. I think, though, that we should have tried harder to increase the score. We should have scored on at least two more occasions.

My ten points brought my aggregate for my three appearances at Athletic Park, Wellington, to fifty, a matter of personal satisfaction. Our two-one lead in the series made us the first British Isles side to win two matches in a series in New Zealand, a matter of some jubilation. Colin Meads capped our pleasure by telling us that we were the best side that had ever toured his country.

The drawn fourth Test at Auckland made the series ours. It was the first time the Lions had won a series in New Zealand – and the first time they had won one anywhere in the twentieth century. We felt – we were – the greatest.

I think that to most of us this final Test was something of an anti-climax, and it will not be remembered as one of the better games of rugby. So much depended on it that the occasion really overshadowed the rugby. Look at it from the New Zealand point of view: the fifteen All Blacks stepped on to that field knowing that they had to work to save New Zealand's face, and that if they failed they would be marked down as the boys who let the Lions win . . . So the tension in this match was different. For the first twenty minutes the New Zealanders played as if they had drunk an energy potion. They were fast and strong and threatened to mow us all down. At the height of this onslaught I thought we were going to be well and truly stuffed. I had visions of a thirty points to nil thrashing. But after a while I saw that their rugby lacked the imagination necessary for command of the situation. They were putting their heads down and running straight. Only the scoreboard mattered. After twelve minutes they were eight points up, but I got a penalty and knew in my bones that we had weathered the danger point. And in the last seconds of the half a try which I converted made us level: the ball went half-way down the line-out, Gareth collected and went off like a rocket. He was stopped, but Pete Dixon picked up the ball and got the try.

New Zealand had no hope of winning, but there were several occasions on which, had we made exactly the right moves, we might have built an unassailable lead. Still, our fourteen-all draw gave us the series by two to one; during our tour we had played twenty-four matches, won twenty-two, lost one and drawn one. We had scored five hundred and fifty-five points and had two hundred and four against us.

Clearly our success showed up some of the gaps in New Zealand rugby. The game there has always involved fierce and well-coached forward play, with plenty of close support, and in the past it has been highly successful. Just look at the record books for confirmation. The trouble was that it became the unquestioned way to play rugby.

Winning the forward battle became more important than winning the game. It is true that quality forward play is the basis of any good team, but once possession has been gained the ball should be used to score tries.

The gain line is all-important in rugby, for you must move forward. This line can be pierced anywhere, but New Zealand coaches still insist on trying to break it as near to the set-piece as possible, regardless of whether the team is attacking or defending. This means there can be little variation, that the opposition can easily counter.

Any player accepts that forward play will be vigorous, but it amazed me during my tours of New Zealand to note how body contact conscious New Zealand backs were. Their rôle is that of support, with steadiness and hard tackling the main attributes, and they tend therefore to be on the heavy side. In Britain it is the forwards who create situations for the backs to exploit; in New Zealand the situation is reversed. And that, in a nutshell, is the difference between New Zealand and British rugby. The Lions demonstrated to New Zealanders that they had allowed themselves to stand still in rugby, that their game was over-coached, too rigid, too predictable and they had not allowed enough room for flair, guile and unorthodox play. We also demonstrated, in that wonderful tour, that it is possible to make a mistake and laugh it off and forget about it, that it is possible to play outstanding rugby and retain a sense of perspective and humour.

Every time I reflect on the Lions tour of New Zealand I get launched into a day-dream: there is so much to remember and so much was packed in.

Pride of Lions

The interest that New Zealanders take in rugby has to
be observed to be believed. It is equalled by only the
most fanatical of supporters in Wales. Three or four days
before the third Test hundreds of people were queueing to
buy tickets – and the queue grew so large that special
queue tickets were issued. Once a fan had one of these he
was able to go away, safe in the knowledge that his place
in the line was reserved. What happened, however, was
that black market operators bought up a lot of these queue
tickets and then re-sold them to supporters at a fat profit.
So many people paid hefty sums simply to get a place in
the queue to get a match ticket. Of course, the black
market is not new – but this was the first time I had heard
of a black market in queue tickets. Many families beat the
touts, though, by queueing in rota: fathers, sons, nephews
and cousins took it in turns to keep a place in the queue.
But it was usually the head of the household who got the
precious ticket. Greater love has no Kiwi boy than that he
sits out in the rain holding a place in the queue so that his
dad can get a ticket for the big match.

As a player on two tours of New Zealand, and as a
reporter during the All Blacks tour of the British Isles, I've
been able to study the New Zealand game and the players
at very close quarters. As I rake over the memories, I rate
Bob Burgess as one of the most interesting characters in
New Zealand rugby. He's different – and it's not just his
ong hair which flows in his slipstream as he darts about the
field. Bob is a thoughtful man, with an outlook on rugby
and life in general that is much broader than that of most
of the men in New Zealand rugby.

In 1970 he made himself unavailable for the All Blacks
tour of South Africa. At that time he had not played for

his country – but he would certainly have been chosen for the tour had he wanted to go. He put his principles first; he didn't want to play in a country that promotes apartheid. In rugby-mad New Zealand his decision to pass up the chance of becoming an All Black was considered by many to be amazing, and in some circles his stand was frowned on.

I identified with Bob Burgess in a number of ways. We have similar attitudes on and off the field. The way he plays rugby tells you a lot about his character. He is not rash and he analyses situations – and of all the players in the 1972–3 New Zealand tour party I picked him to be the man to spark the fires. If anyone was going to show real flair, I thought, it was Bob Burgess. But things did not turn out as I had anticipated.

Of course, there were times when he was able to demonstrate his enormous talent. In the match against Wales, for instance, he showed great tactical control and concentration in one of the best matches of his career.

And, as we saw in the match against Neath-Aberavon, he loves the running game. But Bob was able to show his ability only sporadically. It wasn't his fault. It was simply that he and Sid Going did not 'click' regularly because they were something considerably less than the ideal half-back partnership. They both wanted to be the senior partner and you just cannot have that situation on the rugby field. When he played with Lyn Colling, the other half-back, Bob was always good.

So it was sad that a man of Bob's skill and character had to go around the British Isles showing only glimpses of his real talent. I think that, if he is not given more responsibility and the opportunity to play his own game, New

Zealand will miss a chance. For here is a man good enough to move the ball in an original manner and get away from the stereotyped tactics that have characterised the New Zealand game for several years now. The danger is that Bob will realise that his talents are never going to be used properly and he will simply get out. If he came to this country and was given the freedom he needs he would be sensational.

When Bob, a botanist, came into the New Zealand side for the first Test in 1971, Colin Meads nicknamed him Basil Brush on account of his long and flowing hair. I think it must be something of an honour to be given a nickname by one of rugby's giants. I certainly count myself fortunate to have played against Colin and to have enjoyed his company off the field. I have no idea how many of the stories told about Colin's strength and prowess are absolutely true – the tales about him and his brother Stan, a great All Blacks lock in his time, would fill a book and many are legendary.

Colin, of course, is a very big and powerful man. But unlike so many men of his kind of physique, he has the brain to match the brawn, a well-developed rugby intelligence and cunning. He was a master handler of the ball, great at setting up rucks and tearing the ball out, a perfect support player who knew exactly how far to go in a manœuvre. The cleverness of the top forwards is often overlooked – and on many occasions you had to be close to Colin to appreciate his light touches and inventiveness.

He was a hard and vigorous player, but not a dirty one, and any rugby captain anywhere in the world would love to have a Colin Meads in his team. I remember, particu-

larly, the fierce combats that Colin had with Willie John
McBride in 1971. For one of the central parts of the big
matches was that Willie had to master Colin or Colin had
to master Willie. In spite of the scraps – or maybe because
of them – they were always the best of friends when the
final whistle went. I would say that even in a hundred
years from now, when men are discussing rugby and
arguing over the names of five or six all-time greats, the
name of Colin Meads will always be near the top of the
list.

Graham Thorne was another New Zealander who impressed me: a big centre, an All Black at the age of nineteen and, in my view, rugby dynamite. But, like Bob
Burgess, he was not used properly and New Zealand
missed a considerable boat as far as he was concerned.

Graham enjoyed life and having a good time and,
probably, his attitudes did not conform to the average
New Zealand rugby official's idea of what a player should
be. He settled in South Africa in 1970. He will always be
remembered in Wales for some fine performances during
the 1967 All Blacks tour. Those of us who saw his try at
St Helen's, Swansea, when he made a seventy-yard dash
to score, knew he had an extraordinary talent. The pity
of it was that his ability was not exploited sensibly.

As a fly-half I've obviously had a great interest in New
Zealand fly-halves and scrum-halves. In my time New
Zealand has produced two top-class scrum-halves in Chris
Laidlaw and Sid Going.

Laidlaw came to Britain in 1963, when he was nineteen,
and again in 1967, and was always the first choice. But
as Sid Going's career developed there were plenty who

supported his claim to the scrum-half position. Laidlaw, though, had more to offer. He had a superb pass and could move the ball in either direction; and that was something Sid could not do well. Moreover Chris had the knack of picking the right time to run and he was more fluid than Sid.

I could have played happily alongside Chris, but I believe I would have found life frustrating playing outside-half to Sid. Where Chris was strong and would cover and would take the bangs, Sid usually wanted a bite at the cherry, so to speak, before getting the ball out to his fly-half. It is one of the reasons why I sympathise with Bob Burgess.

Because Sid is relatively orthodox it is not too difficult to set up a defence against sides in which he appears. Stop Sid – and you have gone a long way to containing the All Blacks. But Chris Laidlaw would have played up to such a plan and would have turned it to his own advantage. All this, however, is not to underrate Sid Going. His courage, strength and speed are well known throughout the rugby world. In the Lions v. New Zealand Maoris match, I recall, he produced a magnificent display of rugby – simply because he ran the game his own way, tackling hard, covering, and originating most of the moves.

Another great scrum-half I knew well in the Laidlaw and Gareth Edwards mould, was Dawie de Villiers, of South Africa. Relaxed, yet very determined and aggressive, he suffered many injuries because he was fearless. I would like to have played alongside him because he always ensured that his fly-half had every assistance.

His linking with Piet Greyling and Jan Ellis was often deadly. For these two were talented flankers. Greyling was the destructive one, causing chaos, and Ellis was the constructive partner who set up moves and capitalised on the trouble that Greyling caused. Part of Greyling's strength was his flying tackle: he would hurry an opponent into making a move because everyone knew that he prowled – and struck – like a shark.

I think that the best half-back pair I ever encountered – certainly the finest scrum-half fly-half partnership that Australia has ever produced – were Ken Catchpole and Phil Hawthorn. These men had a real feeling for quality rugby and they were the only pair I played against – they came to Britain on the 1966–7 tour – who had the almost-telephathic understanding that Gareth and I developed.

We were lucky to have the gift of the Welsh language to aid our communication and although Catchpole and Hawthorn had no such secret weapon they had perfect unspoken communication.

Ken Catchpole had the ideal scrum-half's ability to improvise and a very long pass, a long and fast pass so swift and accurate that Hawthorn received the ball 'early' and had the time to make trouble for his opponents. These were hard-thinking men – and I only wish that when Gareth and I had established our partnership we could have played against them. That would have been a great battle of wits.

One of the marks of a great player, in almost any sport, is a willingness and the confidence to do the unorthodox. Frik du Preez, the South African lock, had this ability to do the 'wrong' things that turn out to be right. Like Colin Meads he is a big man and a superbly built athlete – and anyone who saw him during his fine career will recall his wonderful leaping. I can summon up at any time a recol-

A reverse pass when tackled, Cardiff against Barbarians, April 1, 1972

A hand-off. Gareth Edwards hands off Bob Burgess of the All Blacks in the
third Test at Auckland, July 31, 1971

lection of his jumps during the 1968 British Lions tour of South Africa: he went up like a gazelle with perfect timing. In the first Test he scored a breathtaking try, peeling from the line-out and racing for fifty yards. It was an amazing performance for a lock. In South Africa he was without question second to none for he built his game on the hard grounds there, but in this country he was not completely happy. The slippery ball and mud and wet grass created problems for him and during the 1970 tour he did not shine. Still, people only have to mention the Springboks and the 1968 tour and I can see Frik doing all those soft and delicate things that locks, by rights, just shouldn't do, and then picking up the ball and launching himself into the next best thing to flight.

Mike Gibson, of Ireland, is another man with a penchant for the unorthodox. He's a fine utility back and a fly-half I admire. But some of the things he gets up to are most un-fly-half-like. For example, he likes the sordid physical business of tackling . . . I used to dislike playing against him because he comes rushing at you with great speed. But I always liked playing with him. Mike has a natural tactical appreciation of the game and, when he was in the centre, I always felt I was passing the ball to another fly-half. In fact, he often seemed to be an extension of myself.

I appreciate that it may seem, in this discussion on players, that I have been, subconsciously at least, picking my ideal world fifteen. Well, I haven't. Such an exercise may be mildly amusing for a short time, but personally I tire of it rather quickly. Rugby, after all, has evolved and the laws and the styles of play have changed. Players have to play within the climate of their own time and that is why it is difficult, if not impossible, to compare players of different eras. As I've said before, I don't think that my way of playing rugby would have survived in the climate of, say, a generation ago.

But there are exceptions. Full-back play has not changed a great deal in basics between 1904 and 1974, so that it is possible to compare a man like John Williams, of Wales, with other fine full-backs. He has character, guts and style and is certainly one of the greatest full-backs in the history of the game. I always counted it a considerable experience to play with John. Every reporter and commentator of top-class rugby has written of his courage, his tackling and saves. John certainly loves the body-contact aspect of the game, but some other parts of his play are not given enough attention. His reflexes and timing are magnificent: I remember how he produced a try for Dave Duckham against North Auckland in 1971 by simply flicking the ball out to Dave without stopping to catch it. Most men would have caught the ball and then passed it on, but John barely touched it.

His part in the 'golden era' of Welsh rugby needs to be underlined. He knew exactly when a move was 'on' and, just as important, he knew when it was 'off'. His entrances into the line and his cunning decoy runs were perfect pieces of rugby. The subtle things he got up to were not and are still not always appreciated by spectators. For such a big man he has considerable grace.

But, of course, John's courage is something I shall always remember – with gratitude. In the third Test against New Zealand Sid Going was getting the ball and aiming short chip shots at me. The idea was that, as I fielded the ball, I would be overrun by the big New

Zealand forwards. John Williams saw at once what was happening and, because he knew that if I received a severe clout our attack and defence would be damaged, he positioned his fourteen-stone frame to take these shots. In fact, he acted as my bodyguard and took a lot of the blows that I would have received that afternoon.

10. The Last Season

I need to say very little about the welcome we Lions received when we got back to Britain. It was tremendous – and we were treated as heroes. Some of the Welsh boys were fêted in great style with bands and processions and flags and big crowds to greet them. Gareth Edwards was quite bewildered by the welcome that the people in his home town of Gwaun-cae-gurwen gave him. For myself, exhilarated and exhausted, I was anxious only to be reunited with Jan and Kate and catch up on my sleep. I had a short holiday and rested up as much as I could. Then I began training for what was to be my last season.

There was a note of quiet regret in almost every match I played in. Knowing in my bones that I was leaving the game as a player, I looked around the dressing rooms and the grounds that were familiar to me and reflected that a central part of my life was ending, that I would never again be in these places as a rugby footballer. One match I regretted missing was Cardiff's game against Swansea at St Helen's. I always loved playing at Swansea's ground and it was a real storehouse of memories. To my annoyance I discovered that I had promised to go to Newcastle the night before this match, to appear in a television programme, and that there would be difficulty in getting back to Swansea. I worked out a scheme which involved my flying to London from Newcastle on Saturday morning, being picked up in a friend's Aston Martin and driving fast to Swansea. In the end, though, I could not get a flight back and sat glumly on a train reflecting on the match I was missing.

When John Dawes retired from international rugby in 1971 the newspapers started speculating about his successor. I saw an evening newspaper billboard asking: 'Will John Now Get The Crown?'

Many people thought that I would become captain of Wales. But I did not want the job.

It is true that I would have liked the honour of captaining Wales. But I told myself that if the job were offered – and I accepted – I would be taking it just for that, for the honour and a boosting of my ego. And that, I felt, was not a good enough reason.

I knew perfectly well that I had no experience of captaincy. I had last skippered a team when I was a schoolboy. And in the Welsh dressing room I was simply another player with a red shirt, one of the boys. I felt that I was not cut out for the authority part, for giving stern five-minute pep-talks. I thought the boys would have ribbed me for getting above my station.

The fact is that captaincy should never be awarded for long or distinguished service, like a sort of rugby knighthood. A team needs a good captain and captaincy is an art and a skill in its own right. I did not possess it.

I considered that if I were the captain I would play differently. So many parts of my game depended on my willingness to do the 'wrong' thing – but as captain I thought I might feel obliged to avoid the risks that go with that; I thought I might be tempted to play safety-first rugby, with disastrous results.

The newspapers were still speculating and I did not want to be put in the position of being offered the job and then turning it down. That would not have been fair to the man who got the job in the end.

Of course, I did not know whether or not the selectors had my name in mind, but I made it known to sports writers that I was not interested in the captaincy – and that stopped the speculation. I became vice-captain, and that suited me perfectly.

In one way, the last international season I played in was a sad one because the internal troubles in Ireland led to the controversial cancellation by the Welsh and Scottish rugby unions of their matches in Dublin. On the other hand, I was part of a Welsh team that was one of the greatest of all time, and the same fifteen players turned out for each match:

J. P. R. Williams (London Welsh); T. G. R. Davies (London Welsh), R. T. E. Bergiers (Cardiff College of Education and Cardiff), A. Lewis (Ebbw Vale), J. C. Bevan (Cardiff College of Education and Cardiff); Barry John (Cardiff), Gareth Edwards (Cardiff); D. J. Lloyd (Bridgend, captain), J. Young (RAF), D. B. Llewellyn (Llanelli), W. D. Thomas (Llanelli), T. G. Evans (London Welsh), W. D. Morris (Neath), J. Taylor (London Welsh), T. M. Davies (London Welsh).

In my last three international matches I scored thirty-five points and I got eight of them against England at Twickenham in January 1972. Before this match I received dozens of notes and letters begging me to play really well. There's something about the Welsh team going to Twickenham that stirs imaginations among Welshmen everywhere. 'You really must beat England,' one letter said. 'It makes me happy for a whole year when you do.' Maybe all this has something to do with long historical memories, with Welshmen longing to hit back at the English. Also, of course, people tend to bet rather heavily on the outcome of the matches!

I always loved playing at Twickenham, for the English–Welsh rivalry, with the coachloads and trainloads of Welsh supporters, produced a stirring atmosphere. Moreover, the stadium was something of a happy hunting ground for me – and, indeed, I was never in a side that lost to England. One of the small things I treasure!

Bob Hiller put England ahead with a penalty kick, but I made it six-three with two penalties before half-time and, and after that, Wales were on top. John Williams dashed through a gap for a try, which I converted, and I felt that a victory was in the bag.

At the end of every match I always tried to get close to the players' tunnel so that I could make a rapid exit when the final whistle went. It was not that I disliked getting mixed up with the enthusiastic people who ran on to the pitch, but I am not a sixteen-stone giant and the effect of numerous boys and youths smacking you on the shoulders, rubbing your head, clutching your cheeks, jumping on your back, shaking your hands and flapping autograph books in your face can be somewhat disconcerting, if not physically dangerous. And not just dangerous for the players, but for the supporters as well. When I was caught up in these yelling crowds I was very scared that someone would be crushed. If I could not get near the exit at the end of the match I always tried to run off with the forwards for protection. Apart from anything else, I always found that the final whistle was like the turning off of a tap. Suddenly all the strength drained from my body and I just could not wait to get off and sit down.

When the whistle went at Twickenham I dashed for the safety of the tunnel, collecting only a few thumps on the back, and straight into the blinding glare of the film and television lights. This time, though, there was something different. Someone stopped me. Eamonn Andrews was there with a microphone and he was saying: 'Barry John, this is your life . . .'

I hadn't known a thing about it. Jan and the family and all my friends and team-mates had kept the secret perfectly. And those odd telephone calls at home, when people just hung up when I answered, now slotted into place.

I can't say I was able to enjoy the experience much. Certainly I enjoyed meeting old friends, relatives and team-mates. But it was all rather bewildering being on a television programme like this within a few hours of playing in a rugby international. I had to attend a post-match dinner at the Hilton Hotel and there just wasn't the time for me to chat with all the visitors to the show as I would have liked. I remember it as one of the most hectic evenings of my life, with faces popping up for a few words and a handshake, as if they were on a roundabout.

In a way I wish that my last match against Scotland had been at Murrayfield instead of Cardiff. The atmosphere there, with patriotism and Celtic fervour bubbling on both sides among the spectators, is distinctive and exhilarating. Wales v. Scotland at Murrayfield is certainly a special fixture; I went to the ground to see the New Zealanders play Scotland and the atmosphere just wasn't the same.

We beat Scotland by thirty-five points to twelve and our attacking was precise and deadly. I scored three penalties and converted three tries and although I had a good match, Gareth had an outstanding one.

Naturally we felt supremely confident when the French came to Cardiff Arms Park in March. The French are great and they entertained with some fine stuff . . . Pierre Villepreux, who, like me, was bowing out of international rugby after twenty-five matches, kicked two sensational penalties from sixty yards. I had five shots at goal and scored four penalties, to become the highest points scorer in Welsh rugby history. And that was that.

11. In Touch

Sometimes, when I see the teams running out on to the pitch, in the blue and black of Cardiff or the red of Wales, I feel a brief pang of envy. I don't suppose that the special excitement of playing top-class rugby ever evaporates among former players. I'm sure it won't with me. But, as I've already explained, I have no regrets. Instead, I prefer to consider my good fortune. My ten years in the first-class game spanned an exciting and transitional phase in Welsh rugby and in the whole Union game itself. I would have preferred to miss out on this period by twenty or thirty years, rather than miss even a single year of it. As it was, I was at the heart of it.

Rugby has become one of the world's really exciting games. And many more people have started following it because of first-class television coverage and greater interest by the newspapers. The spectrum of its appeal has grown very broad. A housewife who knows nothing about the game needs to learn only the methods of scoring and the fact that the ball shouldn't be passed forward – and she can derive great pleasure from watching a game on television. For the connoisseurs there are the rules and all the techniques – so much to admire.

One of the factors in rugby's new golden era – and the

gold has been of a particularly high carat value in Wales these past few years – is coaching.

When I started in the first-class game training was little more than a run round a field – the full-back joined in simply to keep warm – a shower and a pint or two of bitter. Each club had its own coach who coached in his own way. There was no uniformity. That did not matter much up to a certain level. But when players came together in a national team they brought their varying techniques with them. Different groups of forwards rucked, mauled and scrummaged in different ways.

By the middle of the 1960s it was being realised that this was not good enough. The New Zealanders had had coaching for many years and the pressure for coaching grew in Britain.

People grew dissatisfied with the slapdash training routine which was prefaced with the remark: 'Here's the ball, run around a bit, have a shower, see you on Saturday.'

The Welsh Rugby Union appointed a national coach (the first was David Nash and the present holder of the job is Clive Rowlands) and this was a major step forward. Training weekends and squad sessions were organised and were thoroughly prepared so as to be close to match conditions.

Another great step was the appointment of Ray Williams as national coaching organiser. His job is to create a pattern of training so that, in basics, club coaches teach their players the same things. Thus, as players mature and progress, they have a common grounding in running, passing, tackling, rucking and mauling, and other skills. Coaching is sometimes attacked for leading to too much uniformity and is said to militate against variety and individual brilliance. There's some truth in this, but I remember that this very point was made once to Ray Williams, and his short answer said a great deal.

'I'm opposed to bad coaching, too,' he said.

At the junior level coaching has made good rugby habits national habits. At a higher level it has developed natural talent. I am very glad that I played my last four seasons after the acceptance of coaching. Quite simply it enabled players like myself, and Gareth and Gerald, to make more of the ability we were born with. It has led, too, to the 'thinking forward'. It is not so long ago that forwards were considered in some circles to be not much more than human tanks, just bone and muscle. The new coaching philosophy asks: 'Why not get forwards to side-step and run?'

I must say that no coach ever tried to put me into a straitjacket of his own ideas. I am an individualist and coaches let me have my head – and my own experience is the answer I always give to critics of the new system.

Not that the critics haven't a point. For there is another side to the coaching story. Too much coaching, I feel, can make players stale and, for schoolboys, it can be one of the ways in which fun is taken out of rugby. In New Zealand in 1971 I watched a schoolboys' match and was impressed by the players' skill. But after a while it became clear that they were approaching the game along clearly defined channels and the human element of flair, of spontaneity, was missing. The boys were, in a sense, robots.

They had been regimented and I felt sorry for them. How many boring hours had they spent on the training field trying to improve their movements? Certainly the end product was good, but boys should enjoy their rugby and not stand about listening to coaches droning on about tactics and methods. I cringe when I hear small boys talk of 'going training' and I think that in New Zealand there is too much coaching and not enough fun and self-expression. I hope we don't fall into the trap in Wales.

At the moment the administrators here have their priorities right. They are promoting the game among young people and encouraging them to play. The development of skills comes at a later stage.

When discussions turn to coaching, to the tactics and techniques of rugby, I am often asked to analyse moves I made in past matches and to analyse my own style. I've always found this difficult because so much of my rugby was instinctive, as natural and unconscious as my two languages. But that is not the whole story. There was a lot of thinking, too.

One of the foundations of my game was that I stayed on my feet. Another was that I always appeared to have plenty of time to act, even when hard-pressed. These qualities obviously stemmed from a natural ability but they were improved by my determination to be as complete a rugby footballer as possible.

One of the important influences in my rugby life was an article I read as a boy about Gary Sobers. In this he was quoted as saying that he wanted to be able to do everything that a cricketer should do, no matter what the conditions on the day of the match. He practised hard at being a very good batsman and a good bowler, able to swing the ball and spin it. He practised hard at being a good fieldsman, too.

The philosophy he expressed crystallised all the vague things that were in my mind and fired me with an enthusiasm to reach the same standards in rugby. I aimed to be good on hard grounds and muddy grounds, and as happy in sunshine as in rain. I wanted to be a good kicker, a good side-stepper, a good tactician.

So I developed through practice and experience – and I had the luck to have the talent – an ability to analyse rugby situations and my opposing players. I had in my mind a kind of filing system of players. I knew most of them – and if I did not I quickly learned about them through observation – and I filed away their weaknesses and strong points for future reference. I always sought out the new players in an opposing side, looked to see where they were standing as I kicked off. I aimed to exploit their new-boy unsureness as quickly as possible.

Because I knew many players and teams well, I knew where to place kicks to cause maximum discomfort. I could look at a fixture list and know, three months in advance, the tactics I would employ to upset certain teams and certain players.

From the foundation of a basic ability I was able to develop skills. When I was playing I had a wide range of vision, in the sense that the pitch became a board and the players were chess pieces on it. In a split-second glance, even with the ball in my hands and the opposition thundering towards me, I could spy the gaps on the field and anticipate what certain players would do in the next half-second. The human brain is a marvellous computer; mine was simply programmed to cope with rapidly changing situations on the field, to feed me with the information about the gaps and other men's weak spots.

But that was only a part of it. Equally important was balance. The crucial thing is to be on a pivot and never rooted: to be caught with your legs astride and both feet firmly planted is disastrous, for what counts when you catch a pass is the very first step you take the instant the ball reaches your grasp.

In this matter of balance, one of my fortunate attributes was that I am as good on my left side as on my right. I'm right-handed in many things, but I am a left-handed batsman and golfer. I kick happily with either left or right foot and pass with ease to left or right. This fluency gave me great advantages because I did not have a 'wrong' side that could be exploited by opponents and it vastly increased the alternative opportunities when I was in possession. When I was in a tight corner I nearly always had a kind of back door. And, obviously, the creative opportunities were increased. Pivoted, and in charge of the situation, I could 'matador' – get an onrushing opponent to commit his weight and balance in the wrong direction while I would wriggle, find the gap, pass or kick.

After a few years in first-class rugby I was also aided by my own reputation. Because of my skill opposing players would sometimes hesitate for a fraction of a second before going for me, so that they could assess what I was going to do. This hanging back only increased the time I had to move. In fact, I was given a platform. And, with Gareth's beautiful long passes, the best in the world, I had even more time. Usually, though, I went on to the field with the confidence that I would have a major say in the outcome and that I would normally have the room and the time to do it.

Then there was kicking, always a strong part of my game. It was something I did instinctively and, although I did a lot of practice kicking as a boy, I did not practise much once I was playing regularly in top-class rugby. Instep kicking, which is my style, is usually regarded as hit and miss and, with exceptions, rightly so. When I was playing schoolboy rugby and for Llanelli my kicking was erratic, but it gradually improved to the stage where, if I missed a thirty or forty yard shot, I was surprised. For this round-the-corner style of kicking the ground should be firm. In New Zealand, during the Lions tour, I had the fortune to play most of the matches in good, firm conditions. Even at Invercargill – notorious for mud – we had a pleasant, dry day. There is another factor, too. Groundsmen are more skilful and rugby pitches are much better than they used to be; another aid to the instep kicker.

When the law on kicking into touch was changed some people said to me that they thought my future – I was a kicking fly-half – was in doubt. But their first interpretation of the new rule was mistaken. I saw immediately that kicking would become much more important. Anybody can belt a rugby ball fifty yards. But it is the short kicks and the chips that count, the ability to land the ball, if not on a sixpence, then certainly on a dinner plate.

Accurate kicking is a prime piece of rugby weaponry; it can have dramatic and visible results, such as when a half-back sends the forwards away with a short kick dropped in just the right place, and, on a longer term basis, it can work well to undermine the confidence of the backs.

I always regarded my duels with full-backs as important affairs. No matter how good a full-back is, he can usually be exposed with accurate kicking. If you drop the ball between the full-back and the other backs there will usually be hesitation, a momentary loss of control. I also attacked full-backs by kicking the ball straight at them, hard and low with top spin, making it most difficult to gather. Or I would kick the ball behind them, or place it on their weak side. I would see that a certain player hated having a ball at knee level, for instance – and I was accurate enough to be able to capitalise on this and continue to make him feel uncomfortable.

I remember an attack I launched on Phil Bennett, now the Wales fly-half, when he was playing full-back for Llanelli in a match with Cardiff. I chatted about it in the dressing room and it was understood that every time I had the ball running to my right, that is Phil's left, I would put a high kick going behind his wing and running away from him towards his left touchline. I knew that he would be unable to catch and kick in one step and we arranged for a winger to go very fast for him as soon as I had kicked; if Phil beat him there was a centre a few yards behind to follow up the attack. This simple movement put Llanelli under a lot of pressure and forced Phil into making mistakes.

To any budding fly-half I would say that he should develop his powers of observation and become versatile, building up a large rugby vocabulary. And if he is a strongly right side player he should practise at improving his left side game, otherwise the defect will be exploited. He should develop the sense of responsibility that goes with making decisions and remember that, if he is under pressure, the whole team is under pressure.

He should not be, as I was sometimes when I played for my school and for Llanelli, selfish. He is a link man and a part of the team. This was a lesson that I was rather slow to learn. I had a tendency to hang on to the ball for too long, sometimes to my cost. It is possible to put it down, in part, to youthful over-enthusiasm, but the truth is that there was also an unbecoming selfishness.

To any budding fly-half I would also say that he should enjoy his game and remember there are other things in life than rugby – and it helps if he can play with a brilliant scrum-half.

There is no doubt that the rule changes of recent years have made rugby an immensely better game. And it could be better still if the authorities were bold enough to legalise some of the things that occur in the game that are now illegal.

For example, lifting in the line-out – when a player is hoisted into the air by his fellows to gain height – is illegal. Yet it is a rugby skill and if it were permitted it would add spectacle to the game and would give the scrum-half clean possession. It would, too, reduce barging and fighting. Blocking in the line-out – protecting the man jumping for the ball – is also against the rules but if it were legalised it would add interest.

I would do away with the ritual of the player making a mark for a clean catch. It interrupts the flow of the play and it is not without danger. A player who shouts out 'Mark!' when he catches the ball tends to relax and may not take the proper defensive action as an unstoppable forward crashes on to him. It has no place in modern rugby and should be abolished.

The idea of differential penalties appeals to me strongly. I believe there should be a distinction between penalties awarded for technical infringements and for fouls: soccer, after all, has direct and indirect free kicks and rugby could adopt a similar system. One result of this would be an encouragement to teams, and their coaches and selectors, to drop the thugs who would be losing matches through their violent play. After all, no soccer team would tolerate for long a player whose brutality cost a penalty or two every match. In any case, I think the value of the penalty should be reduced to two points. The emphasis in modern rugby is, properly, on scoring tries.

On the question of on-field violence, I do not believe there is more of it today than there was ten or twenty years ago. The difference is that in the old days players used to crowd together more and the squabbling and occasional punches usually occurred in private. Today the game is faster and much more open so that any flare-up is more easily noticed. In the old days, too, players tended to suffer the odd illegal blows in silence. Today there is a tendency to complain to the referee, if he hasn't seen the incident himself, and that is not necessarily a bad thing. Rugby is a hard enough game and there is no reason why men should have to put up with thuggery.

But if violence is not more severe, the pressures on players today certainly are.

Modern Rugby Union demands a lot of its players and, in many cases, it is asking too much. The changes in the laws and the development of coaching mean that rugby is faster and more exacting. Forwards are running with the ball much more because they are involved in new patterns of play, whereas they used to stand and let the backs get on with it. Every player at the top today is packing much more rugby into his life than his predecessors.

And rugby players, who are, after all, amateurs, lead a harder life than most sportsmen. At sportsmen's gatherings, the jockeys, footballers, tennis players, marvel at the

Rugby Union men who give up a lot, and entertain millions – for nothing. Rugby players have the increasing demands of big matches, of training and travelling, and they have to have jobs as well. Employers, in the main, are generous and understanding and some regard it as a feather in their firm's cap to have a rugby international on their staff. Many players work as representatives because that kind of job normally allows a man some independence and room to stagger his working hours to fit in with the demands of rugby. Inevitably, though, there are sacrifices to be made in regard to family and social life. And the top players cannot escape from the game even when they go back to work. Monday morning brings the inevitable discussions with work mates or customers – which are fine for a while but which pall with seemingly endless repetition.

The public pressures have mounted because the game has become more dramatic and popular, and the players have become well known. There are some rugby supporters who feel that they own the players and this attitude gets on the players' nerves.

I believe that players will harden their attitudes and will be one of the influences that will, eventually, force the rugby authorities to come to terms with the developments in the modern game. I believe they will have to recognise that if a player loses work and wages to play rugby, rugby will have to reimburse him. The Rugby Unions will have to be more sensible about the concept of the game as an amateur game. Now this is, of course, one of Rugby Union's great strengths and traditions, but the authorities are sometimes ridiculously rigid. Players have to be helped to meet their expenses. Everyone in rugby knows this and the authorities should face the situation and not bury their heads in the sand. A little common sense and fairness will not undermine the amateur tradition.

I believe that players will respond to the build-up of pressures by staging a revolt. Faced with fixture lists of more than forty matches, many will tell their clubs that they are prepared to play in twenty, twenty-five or thirty. Only in this way will they be able to organise their home and business lives and avoid rugby fatigue.

Those people who suggest there should be a British Lions team playing in Britain do not take into account the realities of the modern situation: the sacrifice would be too great for all but a small minority of players. With all their other commitments they just could not manage the travelling and training – let alone match-playing – that would be demanded by a home-based Lions.

When I made up my mind, in 1972, to end my rugby playing career, I was anxious to maintain a close connection with the game in my working life. Journalism offered the best prospect of doing that and, when I took off the red jersey for the last time, I signed contracts to write a weekly column and cover big matches for the *Daily Express*, and to take part in sports programmes presented by HTV, the Wales and West of England commercial television company. I left my job as a finance representative and concentrated on a new career.

Reporting matches and commenting on the rugby scene, in print and on the screen, enable me to follow the game with a sense of purpose and with the feeling that I am contributing something. It means that I have not had to drift away gradually from contacts in the game; I also keep in touch by going to rugby club gatherings and by taking part in discussions and sports forums.

To be frank, I do not feel that my future lies in television. It is true that I jumped at the chance when I was offered a sports programme contract, and it is also true that I have appeared a great deal on radio and television and have usually enjoyed it. But there is a world of difference between answering questions and being the man in the hot seat asking them.

I believe in knowing one's capabilities and limits, and not exceeding them. I don't think I have an outstanding talent as a television programme presenter, or 'front man'. I certainly don't possess the kind of temperament needed for long-term television work. A television studio is a tense place – and when the floor manager points to you, you have to speak at once to that anonymous camera. Being the kind of person I am – leisurely, if you like – I find it difficult to work in the tight discipline of the television studio. I tend to be casual about time, but in television you are aware that seconds really count. I enjoy being interviewed and I really am relaxed, but when I have to speak to the camera I get tense and my mouth dries up. I do not enjoy that kind of tension – whereas I used to revel in the pre-match tension of an important international.

Reporting for a newspaper, on the other hand, is a way of life I find more satisfying and enjoyable. I can accept and work to journalistic deadlines, and I love the camaraderie of the Press box.

Jan and I have two children now, Kate and Lucy, and we are happily settled on the outskirts of Cardiff. I do not look too far into the future. People try to book me for events two years ahead, but that always makes me feel nervous and I tell them to come back in about twenty-two months and ask me then. I work from week to week, reporting and writing my column for the *Express*, appearing in the sports programme for HTV, providing comments, assessments and predictions for radio and television sports programmes; I also make personal appearances – presenting prizes and opening shops – and do promotional work for clothes, holidays and sportswear.

I am trading on the name I made for myself to bring security for my family. No doubt the glamour surrounding my name will fade as years go by, though I hope it will always ring a bell among the rugby-minded people of Wales. When I do contemplate the future I like to see myself running a small and not too exacting business, concentrating on rugby journalism, enjoying family life and avoiding formal dinners.

People sometimes ask me if I would like to be sixteen or seventeen again, and just starting off in rugby. I must say that I don't think I would. As I've said, rugby has in my own short time become a much more advanced game and I do not think there is so much room for the unorthodox. I cannot be certain that if I were a rugby 'apprentice' today I would be given the sort of freedom I enjoyed a dozen years ago.

This strikes me as being a pity; sport is enlivened and enriched by its odd-men-out, the players who are outside the accepted practices and do their own thing. These people are the stars, the characters and the colour in sport. I believe that certain basic techniques are important in any sport, but once they have been learned players should be themselves and, if they choose to do things in odd ways, they should not be discouraged. I am a great believer in asking: 'What was wrong with the shot?' when the cricket ball speeds over the boundary. Does it matter if the purists complain that the batsman's feet were not quite in the right place?

The human element, variety and pure pleasure are the qualities that should matter in sport. It is fine to be determined to win, to approach matches with a proper seriousness, but it is a mistake to be serious in a deadly and humourless way. Looking back on my career, from Cefneithin village team to Llanelli, Cardiff, Wales and the Lions, I count myself lucky to have been able, with the help of my friends, to explore new dimensions in rugby football and to have had a lot of enjoyment on the way.

CHAPTER 12

Touchline session: Techniques, coaching, philosophy

I would say that the question I get thrown at me most often by rugby-conscious fathers is the one that runs something like this:

'I want to do everything I can to help my boy become a good rugby player. How do I go about it?'

Frankly, I have nearly always tried to side-step the question. I have had it put to me on hundreds of occasions, but the boys who are the subject of it can be aged anything from six to sixteen – and the reason I usually avoid giving a detailed answer is that I do not believe there is much that should be done by proud fathers. By all means make certain facilities available – have a ball or two in the cupboard, buy some decent boots and be willing to take part in a kick-around in the park. But after that there is not a great deal that even the most enthusiastic father can – or should – do. He certainly should not push his boy too much; he should remember how he himself felt when he was very young.

To state the obvious, environment plays an important part in a boy's rugby. If he is brought up in an area where rugby is the number one sport, the chances of his turning to the game are naturally greater. I would say, though, that small boys should not see too much of a rugby ball, even a miniature one. I hope I'll be forgiven for saying it, but a rugby ball has an unnatural shape. Its unpredictable bounce confuses children and they quickly tire of its behaviour. A round ball is more fun at first and I believe that youngsters should graduate from a round ball to the skills and pleasures that are involved in the use of the oval ball. It is impossible to say at what stage fathers and teachers should introduce a rugby ball into play – but if one is available the boys themselves will turn to it in their own time.

Let us suppose that a boy of twelve or thirteen has swallowed the bait and become a rugby addict. I would encourage any boy at this stage, whether he is a solid and large-boned prospective forward, or a sharp and sinewy fly-weight, to do all the rugby basics and enjoy them.

Although the game is, increasingly, becoming highly specialised, there is still a need for all-round skill and basic grounding. Modern rugby, after all, demands that the forwards have the fitness and flexibility to join in any handling movement and that the centre threequarters can set up a perfect ruck.

The basics involve handling, passing, kicking, running, tackling and covering.

As a fly-half I felt I had to be more than competent in all of them, though I must confess that my enthusiasm for tackling was only a little more than minimal.

Let's start off with *kicking*. Now this is one aspect of rugby that is dismissed too easily. I suspect that many spectators have no real appreciation of the influence a good kicker can have on the development of a game. I always felt that when I was in good form I was in charge; for, with accurate kicking, I was able to dictate how my team should play. It is one of the fly-half's tasks to get his team-mates into the attack and his prime weapon is an assortment of kicks to fit any situation. Any man can clear the ball into touch when positioned inside his own twenty-five yard line – a tremendous belting of the ball will do the trick; but outside the twenty-five the expertise of the kicker will really count for something. And as far as kicking is concerned the new rule about kicking outside the twenty-five has certainly sorted out the wheat from the chaff.

Now we'll examine the kicker's armoury. The *punt* is the most-used kick. Put the boot to the ball and you have a punt. But knowledgeable followers of the game know that the best punt is the one that is flighted, with the ball travelling in a rolling and spinning manner, and not in a straight line but in a curving path.

Control and balance are all-important. When you're kicking, keep your eye on the ball and your head over it. Never toss the ball into the air, but drop it across the foot and kick through it. This action will produce the spin that flights the ball into touch. In defence this kick can be used to gain a lot of territory; in attack, hoist the ball high so as to give your forwards the opportunity to make ground.

The punt can be modified to suit circumstances. With the long diagonal kicks that are used to stretch a defence, the follow-through is restrained so that the lift of the ball is reduced. The average distance for this kick is twenty or thirty yards – and it can be a nightmare for full-backs. I used this type of punt frequently during my career, for it brought chaos to defences. I well remember the first Test between the British Lions and New Zealand in 1971, when their full-back had a miserable time trying to cope with the awkward kicks that bounced and slithered in front of him.

Unlike the punt, the *grubber* kick is an unnatural movement. For this reason it is not used often. But it is most effective when your opponents are coming up on you at great speed and are making it difficult for you to move the ball by hand.

In the grubber the ball is stabbed deliberately into the ground – no more than three feet in front of the kicker. The ball bounces up sharply and is usually easy to gather up again. If pushed harder and diagonally it can be picked up by the centre or the wing. A fly-half or centre threatening to run outside his man has only to produce a grubber kick, and follow up, and he is through the gap and behind the defence in a second. It all sounds simple enough, but the success of the grubber depends on immaculate execution. You need a lot of practice but, when done well, it is an exciting manœuvre.

I need hardly say that one of my specialities was the *drop kick*. Every fly-half must be able to do this well for he, more than any other player, will find himself in situations where it is the ideal way to score. It is a great way to steal three points – and it often frustrates the opposition at times when they think they are well covered. From a set scrum or a line-out a dropped goal is a possibility – but this kick must not dictate a player's thinking: it must simply be one of his alternatives.

In the drop kick the ball must touch the ground at the moment that it is struck by the foot. Nearly always it is kicked with the instep and, of course, balance is crucial.

The type of drop kick will vary slightly according to the

distance you are from the posts and the pressure being exerted by opposing players. When I was close to the posts, say twenty-five or thirty yards out, I usually found it better to hold back the kick for a split second, allowing the ball to bounce a fraction before making contact with the boot. In this way I would get under the ball and so its angle of climb was steeper and it was difficult for anyone to charge it down. With a longer drop kick – forty yards and more – where there is usually plenty of time (but distance is the problem) the contact should be simultaneous, the boot striking at the moment the ball touches the turf. The flight path is then shallower.

When I was playing I always looked for an early opportunity to drop a goal. If I succeeded there were some nice bonuses: three points, a lift for my side, a boost to my own confidence and, quite often, an unsettling of the opposition. I was able to do this several times for Wales – and no early dropped goal was more important than the one I scored in the third Test against New Zealand in 1971.

Place kicking is an art that demands balance and coolness. For many years the accepted way of kicking goals was either the upright or the torpedo method, where contact is made with the toe. Most players prefer this tried and traditional way of kicking; Bob Hiller is a good example and he is perhaps the outstanding exponent.

However, in the past five years or so, the instep, or round-the-corner style has developed. This is the method I used – and stuck to in spite of the raised eyebrows in the early days. Being a natural sportsman I tried to make goal kicking as easy and relaxed as I could. I concentrated all right – but I concentrated on feeling relaxed.

173

I always kept the preliminaries to a minimum; I believe that if you look for problems you will find them. I took all the elements surrounding the kick into consideration as quickly as possible – position, angle, breeze and so on. Then I made myself comfortable. My advice to a place kicker is to assure himself that he is just about to bang the ball over the bar without fuss. What, for a rugby player, could be more natural than that?

Now we come to *passing*. This is one of the game's foundations but it never ceases to amaze me that so many players do it badly. Many tries have been scored through superbly-timed passes – but many more have been lost through poor handling.

Today's rugby demands that all players should be good handlers, that they should be able to give and take passes in one stride without faltering. I'll always remember the way, in a Barbarians and New Zealanders match, that Derek Quinnell picked up Tom David's pass off his toes and gave it to Gareth Edwards in virtually one movement, to help create one of the greatest tries I have ever seen.

The basic pass is to swing the ball across the body. This straightens out attacking moves. Critics have been saying recently that too much rugby is being played across the field. One of the reasons is that players do not straighten up their line; they lose sight of one of the original arts of rugby, to their cost.

Early on in my career I was criticised for being off balance when I passed. I wasn't – but I was very interested in speed. I always told my centres to expect the ball the instant I received it, regardless of whether I myself received a high or a low pass. I made sure my feet were in the correct position for taking a pass. I did not care how it all looked from the touchline or the back of the stand – as long as it was effective and in the team's best interest.

John Dawes would win my prize as the best giver and taker of a pass, and players who have played outside him would testify that with just a deft flick, or by holding the ball a half-second longer than expected, he created hundreds of openings – and saved many awkward situations.

Before a player can even approach John Dawes's standard he must master two essentials. He must have a great knowledge of the way a rugby ball behaves (and that means years of practice), and he must have a mental filing system of the likes and dislikes of his fellow players so that he knows what kind of pass suits each man best.

I always tried to hold the ball in both hands and in front of my body at all times. In this way I could call the tune. When you are balanced you can threaten to pass this way or that, feint and make as if to kick. That way the opposition will be uncertain and you can make them hesitate – and that is often the start of a breakthrough and a scoring movement. Even when you are tackled low there is still enough control and you can pass, or at least release, the ball backwards, as you fall. There are times, of course, when you have to use one hand – when handing-off an opponent or regaining your balance – but the sooner both hands are on the ball again the better.

Although practice, and plenty of it, is important, there is nothing quite like the experience of match play. Many aspects of rugby, like tactical appreciation, anticipation, covering, tackling, can only be improved by playing rugby in sharp competition. So I would encourage boys to play as frequently as they can.

Now to *tackling* – an aspect of the game not always given the attention it deserves. And let me admit, straight away, that tackling was not the strongest part of my own play. A coach or manager ignores tackling at his peril, for while many players can use the ball well they are not so good in the mundane tasks of defence.

When I think of the great tacklers I have known I always recall the performances of John Williams, the Welsh full-back. His fearless head-on tackles have made crowds and television audiences wince. John's total commitment to the tackle is sometimes frightening; the harder you hit them, John believes, the less likely they are to come back again.

This type of man-to-man confrontation is a difficult one for the defender. Somehow he has to shepherd his opponent into a corner before delivering the final blow. Experience counts for a lot in this situation – and so does some knowledge of the way your 'prey' may react to your challenge.

Most full-backs are clever at pushing the man with the ball towards the touchline, reducing his area of operation considerably. Once the man's movement has been limited he can only come inside or kick ahead. If he kicks, then at least your threat has made him part with the ball and anything can happen. If he decides to step inside, the full-back should be waiting, aware that this might happen, and ready to strike.

The perfect tackle then would be to go in low with the shoulder, to hit the man just above the knees. With midfield players, however, the most-used tackle is the side tackle and it is the least demanding. It is used often when a centre attempts to run outside his opposite number: at the moment he is squeezing through the gap and going clear the defender slides himself down his side and brings him to a sudden halt. Timing is all-important and it can be a very spectacular tackle indeed. John Dawes and Mike Gibson were masters of it. They could persuade opposing players that there was a gap to break through – and once they had them in the trap they would cut across and bring them down.

As I've said, I didn't do much tackling myself, but the side tackle usually served me well. I also became an expert at the smother tackle.

In this tackle the aim is not only to stop your opponent but also to prevent him passing the ball. This is particularly important when the man with the ball is close to your try-line. A classic hard and low tackle will be useless if the tackled man has a half-second in which to flick the ball to a team-mate. The smother tackle is the only high tackle that is worthwhile. The idea is to get your arms around the other man's upper body, effectively trapping his upper arms. It is difficult to bring him down with this move, but the important thing is that he cannot link because he cannot pass the ball out and there is usually time for your own players to come round and give help. I always tried to get my smother-tackled captive to face our players: the sight of the forwards thundering up was usually enough to make him try to get the ball away . . .

At the time I'm writing my wife and I have two daughters. Some people imagine that, as a sportsman, I may be disappointed that I haven't a son to whom I could pass on my rugby knowledge. Well, I'm not – and the fact is that I would never persuade any boy, and certainly not my own son, into any sport. I would like him to be interested in sport – and I hope my girls will be interested – but only for the fun they will get out of it, the exercise and the company. I would regard it as simply a part of their education and upbringing.

If one of my children turns out to be gifted at a game, I hope that she – or he – would not squander the gift by becoming dedicated to it to the exclusion of everything else. There are other things in life – and whatever the level of attainment in sport it is not worth much if enjoyment vanishes.

So parents should encourage their children, gently, but should not be disappointed if the achievement is small. I know that some parents' sporting enthusiasm and pushing is a way, and occasionally a slightly selfish way, of fulfilling their own frustrated childhood ambitions. But children have to be themselves, not extensions of their parents.

Appearances for Wales

v Australia, Cardiff,
  December 3, 1966
v Scotland, Murrayfield,
  February 4, 1967
v New Zealand, Cardiff,
  November 11, 1967   1 dropped goal
v England, Twickenham,
  January 20, 1968   1 dropped goal
v Scotland, Cardiff,
  February 3, 1968
v Ireland, Dublin,
  March 9, 1968
v France, Cardiff,
  March 23, 1968
v Scotland, Murrayfield,
  February 1, 1969   1 try
v Ireland, Cardiff,
  March 8, 1969   1 dropped goal
v France, Paris,
  March 22, 1969
v England, Cardiff,
  April 12, 1969   1 try, 1 dropped goal
v New Zealand, Christchurch,
  May 31, 1969
v New Zealand, Auckland,
  June 14, 1969
v Australia, Sydney
  June 21, 1969

v South Africa, Cardiff,
  January 24, 1970
v Scotland, Cardiff,
  February 7, 1970   1 try, 1 dropped goal
v England, Twickenham,
  February 28, 1970
v Ireland, Dublin,
  March 14, 1970
v England, Cardiff,
  January 16, 1971   2 dropped goals
v Scotland, Murrayfield,
  February 6, 1971   1 try, 1 conversion, 1 penalty goal
v Ireland, Cardiff,
  March 13, 1971   2 penalty goals, 1 dropped goal,
                              1 conversion

v France, Paris,
  March 27, 1971   1 try, 1 penalty goal
v England, Twickenham,
  January 15, 1972   2 penalty goals, 1 conversion
v Scotland, Cardiff,
  February 5, 1972   3 penalty goals, 3 conversions
v France, Cardiff,
  March 25, 1972   4 penalty goals

                            Total 90 points

Appearances for British Lions

SOUTH AFRICA 1968

v Western Province,
  Cape Town, May 22
v South Western Districts,
  Mossel Bay, May 25
v Natal,
  Durban, June 1
v SOUTH AFRICA,
  Pretoria, June 8

NEW ZEALAND AND AUSTRALIA 1971

v New South Wales,
  Sydney, May 15   2 penalty goals, 1 conversion
v Counties and Thames Valley,
  Pukekohe, May 22   3 penalty goals, 1 dropped goal,
                                2 conversions
v Waikato
  Hamilton, May 29   1 penalty goal, 1 dropped goal,
                                1 try, 1 conversion
v New Zealand Maoris,
  Auckland, June 2   6 penalty goals, 1 conversion
v Wellington,
  Wellington, June 5   2 penalty goals, 1 try, 5 conversions
v Otago,
  Dunedin, June 12   1 penalty goal, 1 dropped goal,
                                3 conversions

Appearances for British Lions

v NEW ZEALAND,
Dunedin, June 26   2 penalty goals

v Southland,
Invercargill, June 30   5 conversions

v New Zealand Universities,
Wellington, July 6   3 penalty goals, 1 dropped goal,
                                     1 try, 3 conversions

v NEW ZEALAND,
Christchurch, July 10   1 penalty goal, 1 dropped goal

v Wairarapa-Bush,
Masterton, July 14   2 tries, 2 conversions

v Hawke's Bay,
Napier, July 17   2 penalty goals, 1 dropped goal,
                                     1 conversion

v Auckland,
Auckland, July 24   3 penalty goals, 2 conversions

v NEW ZEALAND,
Wellington, July 31   1 dropped goal, 1 try,
                                     2 conversions

v North Auckland,
Whangarei, August 7   1 conversion

v Bay of Plenty,
Tauranga, August 10   1 dropped goal

v NEW ZEALAND,
Auckland, August 14   2 penalty goals, 1 conversion

Total: 28 penalty goals, 8 dropped
goals, 6 tries, 31 conversions
=188 points.
(Some authorities credit Barry John
with seven tries, giving him a total
of 191 points.)

British Lions tour parties

SOUTH AFRICA 1968

T.J.Kiernan (*captain*), R.J.Arneil, F.P.K.Bresnihan, G.C.Connell, M.J.Coulman, T.G.R.Davies, M.G.M.Doyle, G.O.Edwards, C.M.H.Gibson, K.J.Goodall, R.Hiller, A.J.W.Hinshelwood, A.L.J.Horton, K.S.Jarrett, Barry John, W.K.Jones, P.J.Larter, W.J.McBride, S.Millar, J.P.O'Shea, J.V.Pullin, W.H.Raybould, M.C.R.Richards, K.F.Savage, P.K.Stagg, J.Taylor, R.B.Taylor, J.W.Telfer, W.D.Thomas, J.W.C.Turner, B.R.West, J.Young, R.M.Young, D.K.Brooks (*manager*), A.R.Dawson (*assistant*).

NEW ZEALAND AND AUSTRALIA 1971

S.J.Dawes (*captain*), R.J.Arneil, J.C.Bevan, A.G.Biggar, G.L.Brown, A.B.Carmichael, T.G.R.Davies, T.M.Davies, P.J.Dixon, D.J. Duckham, G.O.Edwards, T.G.Evans, C.M.H.Gibson, R.Hiller, M.L.Hipwell, R.Hopkins, Barry John, F.A.L.Laidlaw, A.J.Lewis, J.F.Lynch, W.J.McBride, J.McLauchlan, R.J.McLoughlin, J.V. Pullin, D.L.Quinnell, C.W.W.Rea, M.G.Roberts, J.F.Slattery, J.S.Spencer, C.B.Stevens, J.Taylor, W.D.Thomas, J.P.R.Williams, D.W.C.Smith (*manager*), C.R.James (*assistant*).

Index

Index

Index

Index

Index

Index

Index

Index

Index

Maesteg, 63, 67
Maso, 110
Masterton, 122
Meads, Colin, 136, 141, 144
Millar, Syd, 120
Monkton House School, 78, 79
Morgan, Cliff, 61, 69, 98, 127, 131
Morgan, Marlston, 56
Morgan, Ryland, 58
Morris, W. D., 150
Moseley, 55
Mossel Bay, 88
Murphy, Pat, 105-6
Murrayfield, 74, 152
Mynydd Mawr, 49

Nash, David, 155
Natal, 89
Neath, 56
Newcastle-upon-Tyne, 148-9
Newport, Mon., 63
New South Wales, 124
New Zealand Rugby, 118-47
New Zealand tours, 27, 29, 86, 102-7, 118-47
Nicholas, Mrs Delyth, 98
North Transvaal, 88

Observer, 29
Otago, 103-4

Parc des Princes, 111
Paris, 25, 110
Pask, Alan, 120
Peel, Hubert, 52-3
Pembroke, G. S., 49
Penygroes, 52
People, 62
Plaid Cymru, 122
Pontardulais, 83
Pontyberem, 38, 50, 52, 83

Index

Pontyates, 38
Porthyrhyd, 58
Potchefstroom, 87
Pretoria, 89

Queensland, 124
Queenstown, N.Z., 130
Quinnell, Derek, 133, 136, 174

Radyr, 17
Resolven, 52
Rhondda Valley, 100
Rhyl, 32
Rogers, Handel, 103
Rowlands, Clive, 16, 21, 22, 23, 103, 155
Rugby League, 75, 95-8
Rugby wives, 30, 86

St Helens R.L.F.C., 96, 97-8
Salford R.L.F.C., 75
Scotland, R.F. team, 113, 116, 152
Smith, Doug, 119, 130
Sobers, Gary, 157
South African tour, 86-93
South West Districts, 88
Spain, 109
Springboks, 52, 86-93, 116
Steel, Billy, 114
Stradey Park, 15, 35, 47, 56, 57, 76
Sunday Express, 38
Suva, 107
Swansea, 32, 73, 74, 109, 148-9
Sydney, 106

Taranaki, 102, 103
Taylor, John, 133, 150
Technique, 169-78
This Is Your Life, 27, 152
Thomas, Clem, 29
Thomas, Dennis, 74

Index